Praise for
The Wisdom of a Brok...

"Susan soothes at the same time she illuminates—reading this book, my heart grew three sizes bigger. I have never read anything more helpful or wise about heartbreak. You may find yourself laughing out loud; you will certainly find yourself feeling hope again."

—Jennifer Louden, author of *The Woman's Comfort Book* and *The Life Organizer*

"Susan Piver's new book helps turn the pain of a breakup into a deeper understanding of intimacy. She shows you how to relate to your broken heart with consciousness and acceptance to find comfort, clarity, and balance, even when they seem impossible. After reading this book, you'll know beyond a doubt that you can love again, bigger and better than ever before."

—Gay Hendricks, Ph.D., author of *The Big Leap* and coauthor, with Dr. Kathlyn Hendricks, of *Conscious Loving*

"The body has an innate ability to recover from injury, and so does the heart. Through spiritual insights and practices, Susan Piver's new book walks you through the healing process."

—Andrew Weil, M.D.

"Piver has managed to perform an extraordinary task, namely, inspire a person to want to love again. She knows how to repair the shattered soul, using her personal experience as well as the wisdom of great saints, poets, and cultural elders."

—Caroline Myss, author of *Anatomy of the Spirit* and *Entering the Castle*

"This is a wonderful book. Full of wisdom, humanity, and humor. And it abounds with helpful exercises to turn pain into wisdom. It is helpful even if you are not (right now) sick with disappointment, betrayal, or heartache."

—Natalie Goldberg, author of *Old Friend from Far Away* and *Writing Down the Bones*

"Quite beautiful, a natural read for healing. Many do not realize how much more painful divorce, the betrayal of the heart, can be than even the loss of death. The door closing behind one who has turned his back on you withers the spine, shrinks the boundaries of your life. . . . Susan has done a fine job displaying how the heart's intention can convert pain to growth. How we give birth to ourselves again and again, how we find succor from the 'gift in the wound.' "

—Stephen and Ondrea Levine, coauthors of *Embracing the Beloved* and *A Year to Live*

"Susan Piver expresses in a wise and funny way that even heart-break can become an awakening experience."

—Sakyong Mipham, author of *Ruling Your World* and *Turning the Mind into an Ally*

"Susan Piver understands body-wrenching, gut-busting, brain-whacking heartbreak like no one else. Even better, she writes about the power of romantic devastation with such immediacy and truthfulness that, when she offers the necessary tools for recovery and transcendence, you believe her utterly. I'd follow her advice anywhere!"

—Belleruth Naparstek, LISW, author of *Invisible Heroes: Survivors of Trauma and How They Heal* and creator of the Health Journeys guided imagery audio series

"Susan Piver is an ideal guide for anyone suffering from a broken heart. Spiritually deep, funny and utterly practical, she reveals how this near universal experience can become a gateway to living and loving more fully."

—Tara Brach, author of *Radical Acceptance:*
Embracing Your Life with the Heart of a Buddha

"Straight to the heart and from the heart, Susan Piver is your best friend and wisest guide. *The Wisdom of a Broken Heart* is a road map for how to deal with all the feelings of loss, disappointment, and betrayal. Clear, accessible, this book is for everyone."

—Josh Baran, contributing writer to *Tricycle: The Buddhist Review* and author-editor of *365 Nirvana Here and Now*

The Wisdom
of a Broken Heart

The Wisdom of a Broken Heart

*How to Turn the Pain of a Breakup
into Healing, Insight, and New Love*

Susan Piver

ATRIA PAPERBACK

New York   London   Toronto   Sydney   New Delhi

ATRIA PAPERBACK

An Imprint of Simon & Schuster, Inc.
1230 Avenue of the Americas
New York, NY 10020

This Atria Paperback edition March 2015

Excerpt from Dante's *Inferno,* translated by Mark Musa.
Copyright © 1995 by Mark Musa. Reprinted by permission of Indiana University Press.

ATRIA PAPERBACK and colophon are trademarks of Simon & Schuster, Inc.

For information about special discounts for bulk purchases, please contact
Simon & Schuster Special Sales at 1-866-506-1949 or business@simonandschuster.com.

The Simon & Schuster Speakers Bureau can bring authors to your live event.
For more information, or to book an event, contact the Simon & Schuster Speakers
Bureau at 1-866-248-3049 or visit our website at www.simonspeakers.com.

Red Butterfly © 2008 by Toinette Lippe

Designed by Katy Riegel

10 9 8 7

The Library of Congress has cataloged the Free Press hardcover edition as follows:
Piver, Susan.
The wisdom of a broken heart : an uncommon guide to healing, insight, and
love / Susan Piver.
p. cm.
1. Love. 2. Separation (Psychology). 3. Interpersonal relations. I. Title.
BF575.L8P566 2009
158.2—dc22   2009016132

ISBN 978-1-4165-9315-7
ISBN 978-1-4165-9316-4 (pbk)
ISBN 978-1-4165-9632-5 (ebook)

To Sakyong Mipham Rinpoche,
for his joyful mind, free from doubt.

To Duncan Browne,
for accompanying me on this vast journey
through heartbreak called marriage.
Only with you could I permit my heart
to break open this wide.

And to all Shambhala Warriors:
Rejoice! The Great Eastern Sun arises.

If it were possible for us to see further than our knowledge extends and out a little over the outworks of our surmising, perhaps we should then bear our sorrows with greater confidence than our joys. For they are the moments when something new, something unknown, has entered into us; our feelings grow dumb with shy confusion, everything in us retires, a stillness supervenes, and the new thing that no one knows stands silent there in the midst.　　　　　　　　　　*—Rainer Maria Rilke*

Grant your blessings so that confusion may dawn as wisdom.

—Gampopa

Contents

Part Four: From Brokenhearted to Wholehearted, Learning to Breathe Again—A Seven-Day Program

The Wisdom
of a Broken Heart

Introduction

THIS BOOK IS about how to deal with the trauma of a broken heart, the kind you experience when a romantic relationship ends. There is no other experience quite like this one. For many people, the devastating, obsessive nature of a broken heart is a complete surprise. You have a sense of having been physically shattered, right in the middle of your chest. Discomfort takes over your body, making it feel heavy and dull or oddly light, like something that has been burned to a crisp and now floats in the air like ash. Most noticeably, heartbreak puts your own mind outside of your control. You fixate on certain thoughts or events, torment yourself with unanswerable questions such as "What if?" and "How come?" and are susceptible to shocking waves of grief that flood you without any warning whatsoever, even while asleep. You can no longer count on yourself to make it through a business meeting or the checkout line at the supermarket without having to stifle tears.

Everyone and everything you encounter becomes a part of your heartbreak by reminding you of your loss, sadness, and shame. A colleague's casual morning greeting feels like a snooty taunt; missing the bus is testimony to your having been born under a bad sign; and every single couple in every single song, movie, and television show points out either the impossible beauty of love (if they're happy) or the inevitability of it blowing up in your face (if they're not). The whole planet mirrors your sorrow, and there is nowhere to hide. You once thought of daily events as sometimes having to do with you and sometimes not, but now that the wall between your inner life and the outer world has come down, everything becomes extremely personal and intimate. It feels like the world has turned upside down. It has.

As it turns out, you will see that this is all excellent news.

I'm speaking from firsthand knowledge. Although I've had my share of relationships and varying degrees of sadness when they ended, I've had my heart truly broken only once, and it abides in memory as one of the pivotal events of my life. Although I have now happily moved on, I still breathe in the consequences of this incredibly difficult event every day—but with gratitude, not despair.

When this particular relationship ended, I realized that the aches and pains I'd experienced in the past had been like a summer rain compared to a tsunami. They were not the same thing at all. When other relationships ended, sure, I had cried, hated him, hated myself, and lost ten pounds—the usual. But when this one ended, I didn't just cry, mope, and lose my appetite—my entire world also fell apart. I didn't know who I was anymore or what my life meant, and I wasn't sure I'd ever recover.

When it happened, I lived in Austin, Texas, and worked as a bartender in a fabulous nightclub that featured world-class live blues music seven nights a week. All the legends of the genre played there, backed by a stellar house band. I was in my midtwenties, had not gone to college, and had zero prospects beyond the bar, but I was incredibly happy for the first time ever. Previously, my life was full of icky things like dreadful depression, major academic failures, and painful relationships. When I left home at age sixteen, I moved about in a cloud of confusion and went from job to job waiting tables, driving a cab, and working as a delivery person. Throughout, I indulged a lifelong interest in spirituality by reading countless books but despaired of ever finding a way to integrate my interests and discoveries into daily life. There seemed to be such an enormous divide between who I was on the inside and how my life looked on the outside. But now, coincidentally (and I'm not kidding about the coincidental part—I had been traveling cross-country on a lark and my car broke down in Austin), I found myself living in a town I loved, listening to music I loved, and working with people I came to love. (Shout-out to Antone's: Austin's Home of the Blues.)

Best of all, I fell madly in love with a guitar player in the house band, and he fell in love with me. I had had boyfriends before, but this was different. I had never known anyone like him. He was gentle and smart and funny and also cool and deep. He made me laugh and taught me so much about music. He was a musician's musician, all soul, no hype, hung out in bars but was superliterary with a special love for Isaac Bashevis Singer. He was a Texan with a taste for Jewish girls, and in Texas, I was like ten Jews put together. *Perfect.* I adored him. He adored me.

The first time we kissed, I had an experience that was unforgettable, not just for how powerful it was in that moment, but for how perfectly it christened the nature of our relationship. Held in the circle of his arms, I drew back to look into his eyes and lay my hand on his chest directly over his heart. At that exact moment an inexpressible rush of well-being streamed from his chest into my palm and imparted an otherworldly sense of safety. I had never known such a feeling. We were bound together as lovers in that very moment. With him, finally, I gave myself over to love. Throughout the course of our five-year relationship, every time I placed my palm on his chest, this feeling returned. Even sitting here right now, a gazillion years later, all I have to do is think of him and the feeling returns. This was the kind of love that you can never excise, because you were born with this person already in your heart.

Over the course of our relationship, several big things happened that made us grateful for the circle of safety created through our embrace. I was almost killed in a truly dreadful car accident, and he took care of me throughout my lengthy hospital stay, sleeping in my hospital room every night and caring for me during the months of recovery. A few years later he was busted for being part of a marijuana-selling operation (of which I had had no knowledge) and ended up going to prison for fourteen months. Out of desperation, he had been trying to make enough money to provide for us, something not likely to happen on a guitar player's income. Death, drugs, lovers' sacrifices, and prison: a very bluesy story indeed, with many opportunities to take shelter in each other's arms.

Even before the prison months, however, we had slipped into an on-again, off-again kind of relationship. Although we were bound together by an undeniable soul-connection and the ability to truly be there for each other in an emergency, everyday life was another story. We could not make a regular life together and would break up and get back together, break up and get back together. During one of these breakups, he started going out with someone else and my heart shattered. Into. One. Million. Pieces. To this day, I can't explain why.

I was inconsolable. I lost my mind. I was racked with the worst case of jealousy, which I had had no idea I was even capable of; I had not been a jealous person before this event and have never been so again. My sleep was absolutely destroyed—every night I had horrible nightmares about him being beyond my reach. My appetite disappeared and I shrank to a skeletal size zero. My friends set up a system to check on me, including a feeding schedule as if I were a baby. (Once, three people came over and wouldn't leave until I drank a fruit smoothie, coaxing me to take sips through a straw.) I filled dozens of journals trying to make sense of this pain.

Ultimately, after months and months of struggle, I simply could not get over it and moved more than a thousand miles away from the place I loved so dearly, just to get away from this situation. It helped, but only a little. I am not exaggerating when I say that I did not draw breath for two years without also feeling the pain of this breakup.

Spurred by this utter confusion, my interest in spirituality reached an unprecedented peak. I think I was reading two or three books per week, searching for answers. Why did this hurt so much? How could I make it go away? What was it about me that made this happen? How can you stop loving someone just because they have ceased to love you? All the pain particular to my childhood—thinking I was unlovable, overly emotional, and probably stupid—resurfaced with a vengeance. The pain of today's broken heart brings back the pain of *all* broken hearts, beginning from the beginning. My mind rang round the clock with self-recrimination and shame, and I was terrified I would never be able to put my life back together. I was so afraid. I was so sad.

Then in my readings, I happened to pick up a book that said this:

> This experience of sad and tender heart is what gives birth to fearlessness. Conventionally, being fearless means that you are not afraid or that if someone hits you, you will hit him back . . . [But] real fearlessness is the product of tenderness. It comes from letting the world tickle your heart, your raw and beautiful heart. You are willing to open up, without resistance or shyness, and face the world . . . If a person does not feel alone and sad, he cannot be a [*spiritual*] warrior at all . . .

Oh.

Here was a path that led you, not away from strong emotion but directly toward it; one that applauded the ability to feel deeply—not for its dramatic qualities but for its vividness and intelligence. And if the leading qualities of being powerful and courageous—of spiritual warriorship—were sadness and loneliness, I could imagine quickly advancing through the ranks. For the first time, I read something that made sense. *This sadness meant something. It could lead to something good.* It was extremely encouraging to think that what I considered most problematic about my situation—the overwhelming sorrow and life-wrecking sensitivity—might actually be solutions. Heartbreak could be a source of power.

What I learned from this book, *Shambhala: The Sacred Path of the Warrior* by a Buddhist teacher called Chögyam Trungpa, and from other books and teachers I found, was that a brilliant life is not about being untouched by sorrow but has more to do with relaxing and allowing the world to touch you. It's way braver to open yourself to the world than to wall yourself off from it. I had never before heard such a definition of courage. And I had never heard of a spiritual path that celebrated and invited strong emotion and actually explained how to work with it, not by arguing against it, but by liberating it.

Instead of trying to toughen up, I could appreciate my softness. Instead of trying to stem the tears, I could dive into them and let the current carry me. In fact, the more I was able to own and proclaim my tenderness, the more of a badass I would be. After some thought, I realized it made perfect sense. After all, if you try to prevent strong emotion, you're always on the defensive. If you never put up your guard in the first place, you have nothing to defend and therefore nothing to worry about.

For more than a decade I've explored in my own life this notion of the tenderhearted warrior, of being open to all emotions and becoming strong in the broken places. I've had many opportunities to test and apply the teachings on warriorship. I'm always astonished at how wise, accurate, and practical they are, even for dealing with the most grievously broken heart, and I want to share them with you.

Through my personal exploration of what it means to apply this wisdom to a very normal life of work, family, and boyfriends; of trying to look cute and fearing getting old; of wishing to find home and discover lasting love, I've made a lot of mistakes and also discovered great joy. It turned out that my saddest and most uncomfortable emotions were actually the source of this joy. By discovering that sadness is a form of gentleness, loneliness is a form of fearlessness, and heartbreak is a form of intelligence, I've learned that what I thought were the worst things about me were actually the best.

In this book, I want to teach you how to view yourself in this way. When you embrace what you now call sorrow, you will actually find an immeasurable authenticity and personal power, the kind you've been searching for all your life. Ultimately, I hope you will learn what I have: that by tasting your own heartbreak fully, you experience the joy of owning the fierce depths of your own heart.

TRY THIS

Making Friends with Heartbreak

As you begin this courageous journey of confronting heartbreak and discovering your inner
strength, the age-old advice to "start where you are"
applies. You can't get anywhere without first knowing
where you are. It would be like saying, "I want to go to
San Francisco" without knowing whether you're start-
ing out from Baltimore or Seattle.

So the journey begins by identifying your current
state of mind. I suggest you use your answers to the
following questions to start a Heartbreak Wisdom
Journal, a diary of your progress as you try to find balance and learn from these turbulent emotions. Choose
a notebook or diary that you can easily carry with you.
It helps if it's also beautiful or elegant in some way—
something that feels good to write in. It should honor
the deeply passionate, loving, and lovable person that
you are. You'll want to use this notebook to capture
the random insights that are sure to arise with increasing frequency as you use the suggestions in this book
and face your situation head-on. In addition to insights
and ideas about how and why you feel the way you do,
use it to jot down the titles of books you've read and
what you learned from them, the names of songs that
move you, and notes of encouragement to yourself.
And, if you choose to do the seven-day program I lay
out at the end of the book (and I hope you will), your

journal will help you keep on track and capture all of the potent information that you'll want to remember and refer to regularly.

So, when you're ready, begin with these questions below. Write each one in your notebook and try to answer it. Make your responses as long or short as you like. Don't worry about coming up with some kind of definitive statement—answer each one with the truth as you are experiencing it *today*. Your responses to the questions right now may be different from your answers tomorrow, in a week, or in a year. (You can return to this journaling exercise anytime to notice how or if your answers change over time. You may be surprised at how they do.)

As you review these questions, write down the first thing that comes to mind. If you find that a particular story comes to mind (a moment shared with your ex, an experience from the past, a hope or fear about the future), write it down. Don't be too concerned about grammar or reason, just start moving your pen across the page and see what happens. And don't worry about trying to be all positive. In this book, you'll find no admonishments about avoiding bad thoughts, thinking only happy thoughts, or replacing bad thoughts with good ones. When I was researching existing literature on heartbreak, I found what I named the Cult of Positivity, a dogmatic insistence on turning away from what is painful. This is counterproductive. Without wallowing in pain, we're going to turn *toward* what is painful, not away from it. These questions will help you get started.

If you don't know how to answer a particular question, just skip it for now. You'll have a chance to revisit it later.

1. My breakup occurred _____ days/ months/years ago, and since that time my primary emotions have been _____, _____, and _____.

2. The last time I felt feelings such as these was when _____. What I notice when I compare these two experiences is _____. (If you've never experienced heartbreak before, leave blank.)

3. The thing that has been the most difficult for me since this relationship ended is _____ _____.

4. When I think about our breakup, the thought or thoughts that plague(s) me over and over is/are _____

5. I feel the pain of this loss most acutely when I _____

6. What I miss most about our relationship is _____

7. What I don't miss about our relationship is _____

8. The thing I regret most is _____

9. The unforeseen benefit of this breakup is

   _____.

10. If I could take him back right now, I would/
    would not and here's why: _____.

11. The most important thing I need to tell myself
    right now is _____.

If your heart is broken and you are searching for strength, I want you to prepare to go beyond hating yourself or him or her in order to find the message contained in this terrible situation. Together, we will ride the waves of grief, anger, and despair. You will come to see that during this whole time your worries ebb and flow—but your heart is indestructible.

When I was going through my heartbreak, I did a lot of reading and studying of various ancient wisdom traditions that helped me. The most helpful were specific Buddhist teachings on how to make your heart strong and sure. I want to share them with you, in plain language, in this book. I've worked with them for years now and taught them in workshops, so I've been able to refine my understanding of how they work and how best to communicate them. It is amazing to me how modern and applicable these 2,500-year-old principles are—they are more like an advanced form of common sense than any kind of dogma.

Basically, you are going to cultivate peace, compassion, and equanimity—qualities that are important to help you heal your heart. To do this, you certainly don't need to be a Buddhist (or any other denomination, for that matter). Nor do you need to change or adopt any religious beliefs. Buddhism has no particular deity to "believe in" and follow. You don't have to accept any particular values or ideals, chant OM, wear funny outfits, or love everyone all the time (unless you want to). And you don't have to become a

Buddhist to practice the very healing technique of meditation, in which you simply sit quietly and pay attention to your breathing.

This healing work begins with taming your mind. Without knowing how to work with your heartbroken thoughts—and I'm sure I don't have to tell you this—your own mind will squish you like a bug on a windshield. You're at its mercy completely, and if it wants to take you on a stroll down memory lane or a visit to future sorrow, it will. If it wants to make you believe you're better off without him, damn it, or, no, wait, you're doomed without him, it will. It bounces you around without mercy. To help you learn from your pain and move on emotionally, I'll teach you how to work with your own mind so that you can refocus the dreadful, unending flow of painful thoughts into mind states such as peace, joy, and loving-kindness. The time-honored practice of sitting meditation will be our working basis.

Taming the mind of heartbreak is just like taming a wild animal. First you have to just hang around it in order to demonstrate your lack of fear and aggression. Only then will this wild creature begin to trust you, and you can approach it to initiate a relationship. Meditation is precisely like this. First, by sitting down with no distractions, you enter the ring and do nothing. Then, once you trust yourself and allow yourself to be as you are—without criticism or judgment—you can begin to have a relationship with this wild beast and, eventually, some say over its actions. At this point your situation changes completely and you will have learned to *create* peace—not just find it—and to *create* a state of loving-kindness within yourself and around you. We'll explore all this in depth in chapter 8, called "How to Meditate." In it, I'll teach you a meditation practice called the "Practice of Tranquility" that you can do every day.

Later, I'll introduce you to a second meditation practice meant to increase the amount of loving-kindness you give and receive. Interestingly, the way to heal a broken heart is not just to get more or better love, but to give more. This practice explains exactly how to do that.

In addition to looking at what helps your broken heart, I'll also review what definitely does *not* help, and give you tips and exercises that you can do on the spot, to help yourself *right now* and keep you from habits of mind that don't help. When your heart is broken, no matter how fabulous an explanation you get for why pain hurts, what you really need are things to do immediately when the waves of grief, anger, or fear hit you out of nowhere. You'll find these techniques throughout the book.

At the end is a seven-day program of daily practices and exercises that brings what you've learned about your situation into your everyday life and allows you to change your life into an experience of gentleness and sanity. At the end of this program, you will be in a better, stronger, and more cheerful place. You will no longer define your life as an experience of heartbreak.

This book is arranged in four sections. "Relax," part 1, is about developing some tenderness toward yourself and your situation, which basically sounds impossible when you're completely agitated twenty-four hours a day, even when you're asleep. But by "relax," I don't mean not feeling what you feel. To do that would require a Herculean act of will, which is pretty much the opposite of relaxing. I also don't mean "space out," which is what people often mistake for relaxing. Here, relaxing doesn't mean to stop feeling or divert yourself from feeling; it means that you *allow* whatever feelings are there simply to be there. You will be amazed at how relaxing this actually is, much more so than wishing you felt some other way.

In part 2, "See Where You Are," with relaxation (remember, it means allowing) as your foundation, you will be able to begin to understand where you are, what brings more pain and what brings less, and how you can directly address your feelings. With this information, your situation will begin to cool down and you will discover some dispassion and natural resilience in your relationship with heartbreak. These qualities are there right now, but when you're agitated, you don't remember this. This section contains a number of longer exercises that you can do to help in the healing process. It also covers some very unhelpful behaviors and untrue thoughts, all of which should be avoided like the plague.

"Be Where You Are," part 3, helps you *be* where you are, fearlessly. You can cultivate the courage to meet your life exactly as it is, no matter what, including how you feel right now. Our definition of fearlessness is the ability to open up to, accept, and even take delight in your world, in all the fabulous and insane things that happen within and around you, and even in your own broken heart.

At this point, having opened yourself to the truth of your feelings and begun to take action to view them properly, the wisdom from your broken and unbroken heart will spontaneously arise. This is just how human beings are built. You will feel previously unthinkable levels of compassion and kindness toward yourself and others that you would not have thought possible. You will simply begin to feel happier. You will not need to work at it in order to manifest these qualities—they are simply there anyway. But now you will be able to *see* them as you pacify and clarify your situation. Since you have worked with your heartbreak so honestly, you become aware of an enormous sense of personal power and magnetism that stems from your being authentic at all times. This becomes evident to others, and you will draw to yourself important synchronicities and auspicious coincidences. You completely reverse the terrible consequences of a broken heart—which include a sense of being horribly unattractive and disempowered—and find confidence, ease, and self-acceptance.

Part 4, "From Brokenhearted to Wholehearted, Learning to Breathe Again," is a seven-day program that sets out a daily schedule for working with the ideas in this book to turn pain into wisdom. It includes the things we'll explore together in the first parts of the book: meditation, writing exercises, and other kinds of contemplation. It is meant to take place from Friday to Friday, but you can do it over any seven-day period.

I include this program because it's not enough to gain interesting insights into your situation—we've all read powerful books whose power evaporated once we put them back on the shelf—you have to apply these insights to your life. It's not always easy to figure out exactly how to do this, so I created these very specific steps to help you.

I explain how you can make gentleness your foundation and a commitment to clear-seeing as your path. In this way you establish the conditions for fearlessly owning your own experience. When you encounter sadness, you are fully sad. When you encounter joy, you are fully joyful. When you hit obstacles, you see them as they are; when obstacles dissolve, they leave no trace, and you can appreciate this properly. If they don't dissolve, you can appreciate that, too.

Only by plunging into the depths of your heart can you achieve the self-knowledge and genuine presence that are associated with wisdom and personal power. And when your heart is broken, you really have no choice. Your insides have been turned upside down and your deepest fears and concerns are no longer manageable. You can't run and you can't hide, so it is time to meet them. I'll introduce you to practices that explain how to do this. Even though it hurts like hell, it is a precious opportunity, a clear crossroads. One path leads to a hard heart and the tacit agreement to love more judiciously, to risk less. The other leads to a heart that opens like a lotus flower and, in doing so, connects with an unlimited source of endless, unshakeable love and the skillful means to employ it intelligently. These are the choices. I don't think there are any others.

As we progress, you will discover that the dark power of heartbreak can introduce you to gentleness, fearlessness, and wisdom. If you stay with your broken heart, it will surely lead you down the path to wisdom.

BEFORE WE BEGIN, I want to mention a couple of caveats.

I've chosen to write this book from the perspective of women having relationships with men. So I say such things as "She really wanted him back" or "She was discovering her own strength." This is purely for the sake of simplicity so that I don't have to write, "He or she really wanted him or her back" or "She or he was discovering her or his own strength." This is not meant to exclude anyone suffering from a broken heart resulting from any kind of relationship.

What I'm about to tell you is based on what I've learned and put into practice in my own life. It's very important that you not take my word for anything. Please test out these ideas and practices for yourself. Make up your own mind. What you find valuable and true, keep and use as you wish. Whatever you find that is not true for you, please discard without a second thought. We're about to discuss some of the most intimate things you will ever experience, and only those that resonate on this level will be of use. It's all up to you, so please take this information and make it your own.

I may have made mistakes. I've had the privilege of studying with extraordinary spiritual teachers who have shared their wisdom with stunning clarity and generosity. If any part of my interpretation is flawed, it is purely due to my own lack of understanding, not any error in their teachings.

Part One

Relax

1

How the Light Gets In

SOME YEARS AGO my friend Liz was hit with many losses at once. Her beloved father passed away, leaving her alone with a mother with whom she had a bad relationship. Shortly thereafter, her sister was diagnosed with a chronic physical illness, and Liz, who had just purchased her first home, was the only likely candidate to assume her care; so the sister prepared to move in. Six months after her father had died, her mother died suddenly and Liz had to accept that there would never be a chance to repair this relationship.

In what might have been seen as an attempt by the universe to balance the score, shortly before her mother passed away, Liz fell in love. She called me one day from where she lived in L.A. and said simply, "I've met my husband." Rob was a professional associate who lived in Denver with whom she had been planning an event. One day their collegial conversation about scheduling and promotion had veered off into the personal, and before they knew it, three hours had gone by. They had much in common: both were avid readers who loved mountain biking and the Pacific Northwest and were active in local politics. They felt an inexplicable sense of ease with each other, conversation flowed freely, and Liz felt more and more confident and attractive as they talked. They began to speak every day, first thing in the morning and late into the night. He made her laugh. They admired and understood each other's professional goals. He listened sympathetically to her grief about her family.

When they began to discuss views on relationships, once again they found themselves in perfect agreement. (Two kids, but only after several years of marriage. Separate vacations to preserve newness. Complete monogamy at all costs.) Finally he boarded a plane to visit her at her home. She spent the days preceding his visit cleaning her house, styling and waxing various hairs, and pressing her bed sheets; it was truly like she was preparing to welcome a groom.

They spent several rapturous days and nights together. The ease of conversation continued, but now incredible sexual compatibility was added to the picture. She began to feel that the suffering she had recently endured in her life would be balanced by the arrival of this fantastic man. However, a few days after he flew home, he informed her that, on second thought, he didn't believe they were compatible in the long run and it would be better not to see each other again. That was that.

It may sound shocking and unexpected—and it was. But such things happen all the time. No one knows why.

As the days and weeks passed, those of us who were close to Liz couldn't figure out which loss to comfort her about first. The deaths in her family? Her sister's illness and all the chaos that went along with it? The loss of love? One day she told me the answer. She said, "I'm a little ashamed to admit it, but what wakes me up in tears is losing Rob. I can't believe it didn't work out. What was developing between us seemed more than any person had a right to expect. Our connection was so real and so deep. I *know* he felt it, too. I simply do not understand what happened."

Neither do I. Nor can anyone to whom such a thing has happened—and although devastating, this is not an unusual story.

Of course, nothing can mitigate the profound losses associated with illness and death, but at the same time, I wasn't surprised to hear that she was haunted at night by the unfulfilled expectations of love rather than familial losses. The heartbreak of lost love feels different from other losses, somehow. When someone dies or becomes ill, although we each respond in different ways, we mostly feel varying degrees of sadness, shock, anger, loss of meaning, and an inability to function normally. These feelings can also come into play when a relationship ends, but other qualities arise, too, that are unique to a broken heart: Obsessive thinking. Wild self-hatred. Uncontrollable anxiety and a seemingly irrevocable loss of dominion over one's own mind. Tears, tears, and tears. My friend said that now her day consisted of going from one crying jag to the next. "I can't predict what's going to make it happen," she said. "Every time I witness something, *anything,* of a touching nature, no matter how small—a mom with her baby, people saying hello or good-bye at the airport, soft-drink commercials, for god's sake—I start to cry."

If your heart is broken, this will all sound very familiar. The tricks you normally use to calm everyday worries or anxiety (sleep, books, work, sex, drugs, rock and roll) simply do not work, or do so only momentarily. It's understandably tempting to redouble your efforts at mood control by sleeping sixteen hours instead of eight, working into the night, or upping your Valium intake from 2 mg to 10, but it just won't work. This pain is unique.

When you lose love, the heartbreak that results contains varying degrees of:

1. Insane despair about ever loving or being loved again.
   When a relationship ends, you feel that this one loss spells the end of love altogether. You also feel that it was somehow your fault.
2. Destruction of self-worth, marked by profound concern over personal lovability and, especially, attractiveness and sexiness.
   Very quickly the pain of lost love can also give rise to conspiracy theory–worthy levels of low self-esteem. Things that until recently seemed purely coincidental— a salesperson not offering to help you, misplacing your favorite baseball cap, a waitress who mixed up your order—now seem to be ominous portents of your undesirability, stupidity, and inconsequentiality. Not only is your heart broken, your sense of self is destroyed. For

whatever reason, you feel, because this one person doesn't want you, as if your entire worth as a human being is destroyed and the only way to get it back would be to get him back or to convince yourself that he's the loser, not you.

3. Unpredictable, inconvenient, highly detailed, stomach-churning tidal waves of emotion accompanied by obsessive thought.

   Out of nowhere can come unbelievably powerful grief and an irresistible urge to mentally explore the details of the relationship and breakup. If you hadn't said this. If he hadn't done that. If you had gone left instead of right, not mentioned his mother, only worn pink, agreed to meet his friends . . . you spend a lot of time mulling over your fatal flaws and his, often accompanied by a burning desire to share these thoughts—with anyone. With him.

4. A sense that the pain will never end.

   It is not unusual or unnatural for you to feel that this pain can never end and to be unable to see past it. It is that pervasive and seems that final.

Despair, low self-esteem, obsession, and hopelessness all mix into your life, which until the breakup was basically manageable. The day before the breakup you probably had normal, everyday problems and concerns. The day after, all that was destroyed. No matter how many signs there were (or weren't) that this was coming, losing your love is like having your house and all your possessions destroyed by a tornado. In the morning you went to work and when you came home in the evening, everything you were certain about was gone. It's all rubble. And oddly, unlike a destroyed home that once was there and now is *not,* the person you lost still walks—intact, visible, perhaps only a desk or an email away. He is gone and yet he exists. It is a very strange sensation. It messes with your mind, and the only response that makes sense is to cry.

Our culture generally views tears and what may lie behind them—sadness, anger, disappointment, fear—as signs of a problem.

Something has gone wrong. Somebody needs to figure out who screwed up so we can set this thing right. But tears are actually sweet things. They are signs of authentic feelings. Of course, if you are in a situation with problems, disconnects, and failures, tears can indicate that you need to examine these and strive to set them right. But a good life always contains some sadness. In fact, sadness is a very good thing. Sadness softens the edges around what holds you back from loving fully and freely. Sadness is the gateway to wisdom. As Leonard Cohen sings in his song, "Anthem": "There is a crack in everything. That's how the light gets in."

When your heart is broken, sadness begins to soften you whether you want it to or not. Your normal defenses are gone. When you think of the pain you feel, the tears come. A sad movie or song could make you cry, but so could a happy one; the poignancy of any genuine emotion is inescapably touching. When you see that others are in pain, you cry for them, too. The world actually seems alive in a way it never had before—every moment seems laden with meaning.

This is a precious situation. I'm not saying it feels good, but it's precious anyway. As we'll see, as unlikely as it may sound, in fact this sorrow is the gateway to lasting happiness, the kind that can never be taken from you.

2

Nothing Happens

WHEN MY HEART WAS BROKEN, nothing prepared me for the wallop to the gut that knocked me so far backward I thought it was yesterday. I was a total wreck. I got all sorts of advice from friends. "Drown yourself in work," but I couldn't concentrate. "Don't worry, you'll meet someone else," but I wanted only him. "Take care of yourself—make sure to eat and sleep," but food was like garbage and nights were one continuous nightmare. I tried reading every self-help book I could get my hands on, and although many of them made a lot of sense, once I closed the book, I was back on the couch crying my eyes out.

At around day forty-six of the siege, I decided to throw away all his stuff. It was a hot, sticky Texas afternoon, and I was sweating and crying in equal measures as I took the trash down to the sidewalk. I stood on the curb with the garbage cans and found myself wondering if I could pretend to be trash so the garbage man would throw me away, too. I didn't want to go back in that house where every room was a room he wasn't in. My mind was in utter chaos, spinning out thought after thought: I would never love again. He was probably with his new girlfriend right now, laughing, kissing, feeling fabulous. They were not pretending to be trash, I was sure.

This pain would never end. I was plagued by pictures of my future as a lonely old lady with a girl-mustache who lived in a trailer with many cats and unwashed teacups. This made me cry so hard that I had to sit down on the curb, right there on the street amid the trash cans. The torturous thoughts kept coming and nothing seemed to make them stop.

I can't really explain what happened next. I heard a voice (yes, I actually heard a voice) say, "But nothing is happening." In a flash my tears and tormented thoughts dried up completely. I looked around. It was true. Absolutely nothing was happening. It was as though someone had turned off a superloud television set that had been on for so long that I had stopped noticing it. There was just silence. It was trash day in Austin and a girl was crying. A warm wind was blowing, some birds were flying overhead, and there were sounds of traffic in the distance. Nobody was taunting me. The happy couple wasn't parading about. My pathetic future was a made-up fantasy. Nothing *was* happening.

All the painful and horrendous things I was imagining were not present, and I realized suddenly and completely that it was my thoughts—and only my thoughts—that were tormenting me. If I stopped my thoughts, *the pain stopped*. And so it had. For about nine seconds. Then it all came flooding back, although from that moment on I understood one very, very important thing, perhaps the most important of all: learning to work with the pain of a broken heart was about learning to work with thoughts, not about changing any kind of reality. Because in reality, right this second, now, nothing in fact is happening.

I'll prove it. Wherever you are, take a look around you. What is actually occurring *to you*? Once you take your mind off your thoughts and bring attention to the room or wherever you are right now, what do you observe? If you see what I did, you'll notice that although people may be talking or the wind is howling or you're in your bed alone at night, what is happening is silence and stillness. You can return to this silence and stillness anytime you want. In the thousands of times I've checked since that day, they were still there. This is pretty much always true. All you have to do is relax and look around.

TRY THIS

What Is Going On around Here?

THE NEXT TIME you feel a battle raging in your mind, whether it's between you and him, you and the future, you and yourself, or all of the above, grab pen and paper. Or if you're sitting in front of your computer, open a blank document. Quickly, as quickly as you can, write down five things you notice in your surroundings and be very specific. Use your eyes, ears, and nose. For example, if I were to do this right now, here's what would be on my list:

1. A glass of tea is to my right and it's still two-thirds full.
2. Out the window, it's still dark, but I think I see the first sign of sunrise.
3. The bed is unmade, but since I'm so recently out of it, I bet it's still warm under the covers.
4. A book, *Machik's Complete Explanation,* is on the desk, to my left.
5. My iPhone is charging in my computer.

See? Not exactly the most artful observations you've ever read, but these are the things I notice when I first look up from where I am, which happens at this moment to be a room in a retreat center in Colorado.

After you've made your quick-draw list of five things, now make another list of five things in the environment—but this time take it a little slower. As you look at the environment you're in, try to notice three details you hadn't seen before. Here are mine:

1. The water bottle on my desk has a blue and green label.
2. There's a slight paint scrape on the wall by the closet door.
3. The heater makes a very low hum.

Scintillating stuff, no? Well, that's the point. While a major drama is taking place in your mind, what is actually happening is not quite so exciting. Which, in this case, is very good news. Coming out of your head and into your environment can help cut anxiety for a few moments, and in those moments you have a chance to regain equilibrium.

3

Depression versus Sadness

WHEN FEMINIST ICON and writer Gloria Steinem was interviewed about the grief she felt when her husband died (she had been married only a short time), she talked about her sadness. She was careful to differentiate between this and depression: "I realized that in depression, nothing matters," she said. "And in sadness, everything matters."

When it comes to a broken heart, of course you feel both. But you can begin to distinguish between the state of mind called sadness—wherein the world and all its elements speak to you with moving clarity—and depression, which deadens all sound and absorbs everything and everyone into a sort of lifelessness. In depression, there is only dullness, despair, and lethargy. In sadness, searing as it is, there is life. There is wakefulness. There is receptivity. It takes a lot of courage to be sad. But if you can hang in there with it, you see that it leads to the palace of wisdom and that, when your heart is broken, like it or not, the gates have swung wide open.

Depression can be poisonous. You know when it enters your system. It turns cheery rooms into dismal ones, trifling problems into catastrophes, and small chores into unscalable undertakings.

There is a way, however, to turn poison into medicine. Depending on how it's used, a single substance can be either poisonous *or* medicinal. For example, one extra shot of espresso in your morning latte could give you just the boost you need when you're tired. Nineteen extra shots, however, would be toxic and quite detrimental. Even the most healing substances in the world, like penicillin or chocolate, or kisses, can become poisonous when taken in overlarge doses. It's the same with sadness. When you relate to it in a certain way, sadness increases your sensitivity and understanding. When you work with it incorrectly, however, it can deaden your sensations and make you dull.

Think of depression (an umbrella term that includes any immobilizing emotion or thought) and sadness as being on a continuum, just as poison and medicine are. Part of our work will be to liberate sadness from depression so that you can have access to its curative energies. You could look at what you consider to be poisonous right now—emotions such as grief, anxiety, or anger—as medicines in the making.

The way to ensure that your emotional experience of heartbreak is healing and not poisonous is to examine your intention in working with your feelings. Do you want to become whole so that you can love again? Or do you want to banish your emotions so that you don't have to feel them? An intention that is rooted in a feeling of power, loving-kindness, and compassion is far more effective than one rooted in fragility, bitterness, and insecurity. Paying attention to and constantly resetting your intention (to heal in the name of love) mark it apart from desperation and instead make it the first link in a positive karmic chain.

When you are depressed, you have a limited ability to take the concerns of others to heart. When you are sad, there is no barrier between you and others; you feel what they feel directly and without having to reason it out. Depression is like sitting in a hot room underneath a pile of heavy, scratchy blankets. Sadness is like standing outside with no clothes on. I can totally understand why the former might seem preferable at times. Nonetheless, with sadness you are open, and with depression you are shut down.

An intention rooted in sadness is different from one rooted in depression, usually in this way: A sad intention includes others. A depressed one is usually only about you. When I think my actions will benefit others and not just myself, I find courage where I thought I had none. Holding others in my heart brings an uplifted quality to my actions, and I feel that I am being wise. Acting solely on my own behalf out of complete desperation imparts a heavy, awkward quality, which makes me feel crazier. So, even if you have to fake it for a while (and it's totally okay to imagine you care about others until you can do it for real), try to expand your intention beyond yourself. Let "I intend to find happiness" become "I intend to find happiness to benefit myself and the others in my life." Let "I set the intention to feel no more misery" become "I set the intention to help all beings escape from misery, beginning with myself." You can convert any poison into medicine by applying the proper wisdom. Intention can help turn the poison of depression into the medicine of sadness.

TRY THIS
Include Others

THE NEXT TIME you notice that despair is driving you and you don't know how to believe in happiness anymore, slow down. Pick up a pen and a piece of paper and write down the wish that is at the center of your desperation: "I will find love again, I will, I will," or, "There *has* to be someone out there for me." Then look at what you've written. It's likely that your strongest feeling is fear—a fear that if you don't find love again you will feel bereft, empty, alone. This fear makes you cling harder and harder. Change it by imagining that your wish comes true and, once it *has* come true, you'll be in a much better position to help others, either someone specific or people in general. Rewrite your wish so that it includes others. "I will find love again so that I can be strong enough to make the world a better place." Make finding happiness a crusade on behalf of more than yourself. This is a great way to relax the awful anxieties you're feeling and find some energy to move out of sadness and depression and to keep moving forward.

4

Completely Uncool

Love's happiness is just an illusion
Filled with sadness and confusion.

—Jimmy Ruffin, *What Becomes of the Brokenhearted*

IF YOU EVER HAD a shred of belief that you were in any way cool, you can forget about that now that you have a broken heart. Maybe you prided yourself on having great taste in art, superior communication skills, or a slamming wardrobe. Perhaps you were confident that you were hipper than 99 percent of the people on the planet when it came to understanding the fine points of reggae music/Manhattan restaurants/social networking/anime. Suddenly, none of these things matters. There is nothing cool about you, nothing whatsoever. Heartbreak has a way of doing that to a person.

It's hard to be cool when you feel so pathetic, desperate, and lonely that you don't even care about things you used to get excited about. Where once you may have enjoyed parties for the chance to schmooze or smirk, or you considered the other people waiting for the bus as nuisances who might take your seat, now you want to grab everyone you meet, sob your story to them, and beg them to show mercy. It's impossible to believe that the world and its inhabitants could simply . . . go on, especially in the face of the enormity of your grief.

Surprisingly, every single cliché that you have ever heard about lost love turns out to be true. You *can't* believe life around you goes on as before. You feel that you can't exist without this person. Life has lost its meaning. You've been sucked into a giant black hole from which you feel you can never escape. You are certain you will never love again. Songs, movies, and stories you may have branded as childish and sentimental now capture your feelings perfectly. You never knew you could have such affinity for Céline Dion or Lifetime Television. It's pretty humbling.

It's also pretty great. You can forget about keeping up your standing in whatever in-group you count yourself a member of, because now you know that it simply doesn't matter. Heartbreak is the great leveler and an amazing antidote to B.S., your own and others'. Age-defying face creams, the latest "it" bag, or tidbit of celebrity gossip, while perhaps still delicious, leave you largely unmoved. You abruptly find yourself outside the realm of the mainstream and its advertisements. No one and nothing can hype you.

"There's going to be a seismic change. I think it's the end of the age of irony," announced Graydon Carter, editor of *Vanity Fair* magazine in the days after September 11. "Things that were considered fringe and frivolous are going to disappear." This may have happened for a few weeks or months, but then things pretty much went back to normal. But during those weeks and months there was a spontaneous and heightened love for our country and one another. It was pretty amazing.

I'm not intending to compare your relationship with the tragedies of 9/11 but a truly shattering event pierces all veils of style and pretense. In its wake, you realize that the little things that once made you feel safely ensconced with the cool people who are in the right (supporting universal healthcare or knowing that T-Bone Walker was the king of Texas guitar or preferring the U.K. *What Not to Wear* over the U.S. *What Not to Wear* or vice versa) are revealed for what they are: inconsequential. They have nothing to do with what makes life worth living. In fact, looking back on how vehemently you may have defended certain positions or raged against those who thought or acted differently from you can now seem a little embarrassing. It just doesn't matter. When your heart is broken, along with the pain comes an unmistakable ability to know what matters and what doesn't. Only love matters, you think. This, by the way, is true and now, courtesy of your broken heart, you know it beyond a shadow of a doubt.

TRY THIS

Question Your Reality

COMPARING YOUR PRE-BREAKUP to post-breakup life, answer these questions in your Heartbreak Wisdom Journal.

Before this relationship ended:

1. I believed that my most important problems were:

2. My closest friends were:

3. I spent most of my spare time:

4. My number one aspiration was:

5. I ranked my priorities as follows (place a number by each priority; add ones that may be missing):

_____ Career/School

_____ Family

_____ Friends

_____ Health

_____ Money

_____ Romance

_____ Self-Discovery

_____ Spirituality

Now that this relationship has ended:

6. I believe that my most important problems are:

7. My closest friends are:

8. I spend most of my spare time:

9. My number one aspiration is:

10. I rank my priorities as follows (place a number by each priority; add ones that may be missing):

_____ Career/School

_____ Family

_____ Friends

_____ Health

_____ Money

_____ Romance

_____ Self-Discovery

_____ Spirituality

What, if anything, do you notice about how your concerns, friendships, and priorities have shifted—or not? Has the breakup caused any shifts that really trouble you? Delight you? Surprise you? Or has everything basically remained the same? Visit these questions once a week for a while and write any observations in your journal.

5

It Is a Dark Night

HEARTBREAK PRESENTS a very important choice: you can either open to it and allow it to soften and strengthen you, or you can fight it tooth and nail and turn away from it, which is tantamount to giving it permission to harden your heart. There really are no other choices. Far more than mere fodder for movies and pop songs, a broken heart is a dark night of the soul, let there be no mistake about it.

At one time or another, most people experience this dark night, which can be brought about by any sudden, catastrophic loss, betrayal, or illness. In Spain in the sixteenth century, the Carmelite monk Saint John of the Cross wrote his extraordinary poem *Dark Night of the Soul* to describe the transformation that the soul goes through by enduring pain, abandonment, and suffering. On the other side of the pain is a greater understanding, insight, and full maturity.

A Dark Night can last a lot longer than eight hours of darkness. It's a mental and emotional state of despair that arises when something is so painful that it blots out all other considerations and makes carrying on as usual out of the question. You look at your colleagues, friends, and strangers and know that you inhabit a different world than they do, one where there is no "normal." You are compelled to look beyond the commonplace to seek a greater meaning in your life, something that connects one event to another and provides some sense. Loss torches the boundaries of your safe, small world and forces you into a larger view.

You're in a Dark Night when you realize there is no way around your condition. You can't fix it, reverse it, or ignore it. The only way out is through. You can allow yourself to go through it and accept that you have to go through and let it change you, or you can fight it and become emotionally and spiritually hardened. Unfortunately, there do not appear to be other choices.

For many people, a broken heart is the sudden gateway into this profound state of mind. You may not like it, but the Dark Night plunges you into conversation with life's most pressing questions: Who am I? What am I doing with my life? How can what I most desire (love) be also what is most treacherous? Losing love refocuses all of your attention away from intellectual, physical, or professional concerns and places it instead on love itself, to beg perhaps the most critical question of all: How can I permit myself to love when the possibility of loss cannot be denied? These now become the most important questions in the world and they demand exploration.

Such an exploration requires a mind-set that may be very different from the one you use to solve conventional problems. In fact, thinking about the Dark Night as a problem to be solved could create more pain and confusion. Sadness and grief this big are not mistaken reactions that you can clear up by employing the correct diagnostic and applying the recommended solution. The feelings you're experiencing are the right response to the loss of love, whether or not your friends, family, inner critic, *Cosmo* magazine, or pop psychologists agree. Simply acknowledging your emotional state as appropriate (even if you don't understand why it is—yet) helps you find an element of spaciousness in a very claustrophobic situation. This is good. Now you have some room to explore. So begin with the recognition that, no matter how huge and uncomfortable your feelings, they are also accurate and in accord with a mysterious inner logic.

A Dark Night of the Soul is not the universe's attempt to rob you of happiness or beat you into submission—on the contrary. It is a natural cycle of life that teaches you the meaning of happiness beyond pleasure. It offers the opportunity for liberation from inauthenticity. If you acknowledge the Dark Night and open to it, it will teach you extraordinary lessons about who you are and what your life is about. What those lessons are, I cannot tell you because they will be unique to you, completely personal. All I can say is that the moment you do open yourself to a Dark Night, tremendous inner wisdom will come to your aid in the guise of sudden insights and auspicious coincidences.

No psychological strategy will help; this is a spiritual enterprise, and therefore tools such as analysis of family history, dissection of prior relationships, affirmations, and behavioral modifications, though interesting, will not carry you far enough. Spiritual qualities such as allowing things to be as they are, tolerance for not understanding your feelings, faith in basic goodness, and an attraction to what is mysterious and shadowy in your life will be far more useful. Opening to darkness means to feel what you are feeling, minus the story behind it, minus explanations for how to escape, and minus the tyranny of positive self-talk.

No matter how much help you ask for, cultivating these spiritual qualities is something you have to do within yourself, and it requires solitude. So if you feel like locking your door, closing the blinds, and retreating from the world, this is probably a good idea. Sit with the darkness. Allow it to teach you. This is a very brave thing to do.

It starts with the realization that a broken heart is nothing to be ashamed of. It is an altered state, an experience of sacred openness. When you are in this state, you walk with poets, saints, and revolutionaries—anyone who has ever been forced out of his or her customary life by sudden loss and was made stronger by it. These great souls are your compadres now, and they include our greatest poets, sages, musicians, and artists. Identify your own brothers and sisters of the Dark Night. They're definitely out there. Ask yourself: Of the songwriters, painters, saints, and revolutionaries I know of, which ones experienced what I am experiencing now and returned to teach about it? Whose art or life expresses what I feel? Who has encountered the Dark Night and faced it with the kind of courage and openness I aspire to?

History, mythology, literature, art, and music are full of figures who can guide us through darkness, who have mapped its subtleties—the patron saints of the night, of gloom and melancholy. Read their stories, study their work, and listen to their songs. Persephone, Milarepa, Saint John of the Cross, John Donne, Dante, Rainer Maria Rilke, Rabindranath Tagore, Muddy Waters, Chögyam Trungpa, Ingmar Bergman, Leonard Cohen, Willie Nelson, Pema Chödrön, Thomas Moore; these are heroic explorers of the shadows and they have much to teach me about joy.

When you find your patron saints of the dark, examine their lives. Gather tokens of their existence and place them in your home or carry them with you. Evoke them in your mind when you are despairing. Imagine that they walk with you. When I was going through the most despairing period of my own broken heart, I journaled perhaps a hundred zillion times a day about the deepest, darkest depths I encountered. As I sat down to write, I would invoke the spirits of my personal dark saints: Emily Dickinson, Isak Dinesen, Blind Willie Johnson, Bob Dylan, Billie Holiday, Bruce Springsteen. Although all very different, each of them displayed through his or her art the willingness to open to heartbreak and be respectful of its sorrow. All had the courage to enter into the shadows and express what they found. I am so grateful to them. Each guided me through the dark terrain and back again.

Although it is tremendously disorienting on one hand, on another, you will never see as clearly as you do when your heart is broken. If you've ever wanted to get at the truth about your life, your character and destiny, the depth of your friendships, you can choose to see these things now.

When I woke up in a hospital room after my devastating car accident, I didn't yet have a broken heart (broken ribs—even around the heart—don't count), but as with heartbreak, my world had suddenly been reduced to breath and bone. I was immobilized, studded with tubes, and surrounded by the sound of machinery measuring my bodily functions. Life as I knew it had ceased to be. How did I look? I didn't care. Did people like me? I couldn't remember. How much money had I managed to save? Did my boss appreciate my work? Would I get invited to this party or that professional association? These questions suddenly seemed ridiculous, completely pointless. Everything I needed to know was obvious. Each inhalation was good and so was each exhalation. Pain hurt. No—pain didn't. Whenever anyone, friend, doctor, or nurse, visited me, I was able to take them in completely: their eyes, their voice, their nervousness, their caring. I saw who was capable of facing difficult situations and who was not. I saw who was open to me and who was closed.

I had many surprises. People I would have guessed were stalwart friends disappeared from my life and those I hadn't noticed before came forward out of nowhere to care for me. Every expression of love went so deep and affected me so much. Although the pain and uncertainty were enormous, I couldn't help but notice that along with this devastation had come a giant, infallible bullshit meter. Without having to think about it, I saw who and what was important without the filters of conventional thought.

In the middle of this crazy situation I also felt confident and at ease in a way I had never before experienced. I'm not saying I felt comfortable or cheery; in fact, I was rather cranky. But in some way, clarity and a bizarre sort of peace marked my months in the hospital. (And I don't think that's the morphine talking . . .) When you look back on your days, weeks, or months of heartbreak, I predict you will find the same thing: that this is a time of clear-seeing and accurate insight, a period where the truth of all your relationships, aspirations, and priorities becomes immediately, crushingly, undeniably apparent.

Again, I have to tell you that you can give in to the Dark Night or try to resist it. It is not easy to give in, but it is necessary. And it's actually a simple choice. What you now consider emotional self-defense or protecting your heart—crying out for your lover to come back, pinning the blame on something or someone, or urging yourself to move past it already—actually sets you back. And what may look like giving in—crying without reason, letting the pain touch you fully, and inviting yourself to be present to your heartache, moment by moment—is actually what heals.

TRY THIS
Finding Friends in the Dark

CHOOSE TWO OR THREE BOOKS or songs by people who have demonstrated familiarity with the kind of despair you're experiencing. Keep them somewhere accessible and, when you feel that you are about to drown in darkness, turn to one of them. Try to find the line, passage, or chapter that expresses most clearly what you feel right now. Get out your Heartbreak Wisdom Journal and copy the salient lines into it. Describe in a few sentences or paragraphs how or why these particular lines pierce you to the core. See if you can rewrite the lines in your own words and make your own poetry. Or you could write a letter to the author or songwriter, explaining your situation and thanking him for his work.

If you don't know where to begin, you could always start with this passage:

> Midway along the journey of our life
> I woke to find myself in a dark wood,
> for I had wandered off from the straight path.
> How hard it is to tell what it was like,
> this wood of wilderness, savage and stubborn
> (the thought of it brings back all my old fears),

> *a bitter place! Death could scarce be bitterer.*
> *But if I would show the good that came of it*
> *I must talk about things other than the good.*
>
> —DANTE, *INFERNO*, CANTO 1 (Transl.: Mark Musa)

And try this, too: Periodically open your journal and write the answers to these questions. Think of them as a kind of Dark Night of the Soul Mad Libs:

If my sadness could speak, what it would tell me today is: _____.

Before the breakup, I would describe my three best qualities as _____, _____, and _____. Now I would say they are _____, _____, and _____.

Before the breakup, I would describe the three most essential qualities in a life partner as _____, _____, and _____. Now I would say they are _____, _____, and _____.

The person I would most like to discuss my broken heart with is _____. The question I would ask him or her is: _____. What I would hope to learn is _____.

Oh yes, and you could also try this: Once when I was attending a month-long meditation retreat, a student asked our teacher a question about mental agitation during meditation. The student was becoming frustrated that, two weeks into the retreat, he was still experiencing wave after wave of such difficult emotions as frustration, anxiety, and irritation. No matter how much he tried to relax, he kept his cranky pants on. "You could offer your negativity to the deities," our teacher said, pointing to pictures on the shrine of the gods and goddesses of compassion, wisdom, and peace. "They love the display."

The teacher wasn't suggesting that we pray to an external deity. (But if you want to, you may try.) In Buddhism, pictures or statues of gods and goddesses represent nothing more (or less) than your own wisdom mind. The point is to give your pain away to whatever you believe in, not to offload it, but to wish that somehow what you are experiencing could benefit others. Believe me, I don't know how my petty grievances or monumental heartaches could be spun into gold for the sake of others, but whenever I focus in on a difficult feeling, close my eyes, and think, "I offer it," I feel liberated and uplifted.

Try it. When you are in the pits of despair, stop. Tune in to what you admire or respect most: it could be God, Jesus, a saint, Mother Nature, quantum physics, the power of love, or your own highest wisdom. Whatever it is, offer it your sorrow, your rage, your fear, your hatred, with the wish that whoever or whatever is on the receiving end will enjoy the display of color, light, and life—and somehow put it to good use.

6

Making Friends with Heartbreak

A FEW MONTHS AFTER my longtime boyfriend and I had broken up, I was charged with conducting a business meeting at a restaurant over lunch. I was pretty sure I was on the road to recovery and had been genuinely looking forward to this opportunity to discuss an exciting new project with the other attendees, colleagues I respected and admired. I made a reservation at a favorite restaurant that we had been to many times before where the food was always delicious. *Yes,* I thought, *I'm going to be okay. I have a good job I work with wonderful folks. Our meeting is going to be fun. I am moving on, damn it.*

So I drove to the meeting with a lovely feeling of things returning to normal. The seven of us, as I had requested, were seated at the only round table in the restaurant large enough to accommodate a group of that size. We were settling ourselves around the table, waving hello, pulling out papers, and turning off cell phones, when everything completely fell apart for me. *The waiter had brought us a basket of jalapeño cheddar-cheese corn bread.*

Oh no. *He* loved jalapeño cheddar-cheese corn bread. A mere glimpse of those crumbly, orangey squares flecked with green blotted out all feelings of normality and, once again, my world turned upside down. Tears stung the backs of my eyeballs, and I gruffly pushed away my chair to try to make it to the ladies' room, but not quite in time—the tears had already begun to fall. *There's no hope,* I thought. Just when I thought I was getting my life back, a piece of bread caused it to disintegrate once again. I sat down in one of the stalls and tried to cry without making any noise, which, as anyone who has attempted this knows, only leads to a bulbous nose and a Mount Rushmore–size headache. Somehow I soldiered on and made it through the meeting, and when I got home at the end of the day, I was too tired to cry anymore so I just lay on the couch. For about six hours. When I finally dragged myself to bed, I thought, *I'll never get over this. Why? Why do the waves of grief just keep coming? What is happening here, and will it ever end?*

At this point I realized that there was very little, maybe nothing, I could do to predict, modulate, and manage these unpredictable waves of grief. Trying to fight them would be like trying not to have nightmares by staying awake all night just in case one might arise. It was just too exhausting. I had to accept that these episodes were simply a part of my life for the time being and I was going to have to learn to deal with them instead. But how?

Soon after this, I was attending a talk at a local meditation center by a Tibetan Buddhist monk. He was young, not yet thirty, but already highly respected as a scholar and spiritual adept. After talking about overcoming obstacles such as depression and anxiety, he was asked about how we can manage our emotions in a world of ever-increasing danger and uncertainty, how to cope with feelings of paralyzing dread about our safety and the future of the planet. The monk said, "When you are filled with fear, anxiety, or other difficult emotions, the first thing you should always do is make friends with them."

Rather than fighting off unpleasant feelings, it is always best to soften, open, and invite them. Fighting wastes valuable time. Allowing them acknowledges the reality of that particular moment and makes it easier to address your circumstances intelligently. For example, if you're walking down a dark street trying to pretend you're not afraid, you might miss the valuable signals fear offers you when you tune in and open to it.

And so it is with a broken heart, or any other problem, really.

You may have been taught to attack a problem when you encounter it, either by trying to fix it right away or else eradicating it. I'm not suggesting that this is never a good idea, but there is another option that is not often thought of, which is to extend the hand of friendship to your situation. This is an extraordinary thing to do. Making friends with your broken heart—instead of trying to mend it or banish it—begins by simply making room for it to exist.

You could even invite it to sit down with you since you've probably been hating it or trying to ignore it. When grief and disappointment threaten to overwhelm you, instead of bemoaning them, turning away, or shrinking in fear of them, you could feel them. Instead of trying to shout them down either by talking yourself out of what you're feeling (It's all his fault anyway), making up a story about what it all means (I always attract the wrong guys), or collapsing on the couch with a bottle of gin (to deaden the pain), invite in your feelings and get to know them.

For example, when you feel grief, where does it manifest in your body? Does it weigh down your chest, close your throat, or make your shoulders ache? How about disappointment or anger or any of the other feelings that have become your companions? If your emotion had a color, what would it be? If your emotion could speak to you (instead of the other way around), what would it say? When you suddenly feel a pang of emotion, positive or negative, can you go back and pinpoint the exact moment it arose? These are useful questions. Just like getting to know a new friend, the first step is simply to find out about her.

This process is really, really hard, so you need to appreciate yourself and what you are going through. So many problems result from the inability to simply be kind to yourself. Please develop some sympathy for yourself, which is different from self-pity or self-indulgence. Imagine if you knew that your best friend or your child or your mom was going through what you are experiencing—wouldn't your heart ache for her? Wouldn't you feel that if only there was something you could do to help, you would do it? Wouldn't you think about her night and day with kindness, hoping for her to find peace?

Ask yourself honestly: have you felt these things about yourself?

If you have, that is wonderful; you are a great friend. If you haven't, you could try to offer kindness to yourself. You know that the ultimate kindness, the best thing you can do for a friend, is simply to be there with her and for her when she's falling apart. Offering advice is not helpful unless you've been asked directly to give it. You know that trying to talk her out of what she's feeling or convince her that it's not a big deal is unkind. Telling her to buck up already is certainly not helpful. What helps more than anything? Simple, unquestioning, ultrapatient companionship. Be by her side. Take her to a movie to get her mind off the situation. Check in with her throughout the day just so she'll know someone is thinking of her. Listen to her patiently, no matter how many times you've heard the story; feel sad with her when she cries and relieved when her spirits begin to rise.

What helps more than anything is to be gentle toward yourself. Gentleness doesn't mean being all "poor baby" or coddling yourself in any way. Real gentleness has way more precision and intelligence than that. Gentleness means simply that you acknowledge and embrace your own experience from moment to moment, without judgment. Without trying to fix it. Without feeling ashamed of it or, if you do feel ashamed of it, you do not feel ashamed of your shame! In this way, gentleness is actually an advanced form of bravery. You aren't afraid to take on your own suffering, even though you don't know how or when it will end; still, you agree to feel it. Somehow this acceptance begins to calm things down. On its own timetable, gentleness begins to pacify even the most raging emotions. Gentleness is the spiritual and emotional warrior's most powerful weapon.

The best way to cultivate gentleness toward yourself, thought by thought and moment by moment, is through the sitting practice of meditation. In fact, meditation, which is sitting with your self, your thoughts, emotions, and yearnings, and simply allowing them to be as they are, *is* the practice of gentleness itself. There is no better teacher than this.

Most likely, there will be only a few times in your life when you'll reach the limit of what you can bear. It may be from falling ill, the death of a parent, or even the loss of a most precious possession, such as your home, and of course it can also be because of a broken heart. To face these extraordinary times, you need to take extraordinary measures. Most of the tactics touted as "extraordinary measures," however, are really ways of escaping the reality of what we must face: our emotions. Certainly drinking, drugging, random sex, and sleeping all the time are ways to avoid emotional pain, but even healthier means, such as positive thought, physical exercise, therapy, or simply forcing yourself to move on, are also methods of stepping *away* from what ails you, rather than toward it. Stepping toward it and going into it do not just mean lying around crying all the time. It means meeting your emotions and relating to them, not as enemies to be conquered, but as wounded friends from the front, needing your loving attention.

TRY THIS

Ninety-Second Clarity Exercise

THE FIRST STEP in not letting difficult emotions freak you out is to relax with them. This does *not* mean that you stop feeling agitated. I recognize this sounds contradictory! How can you relax and feel agitated at the same time? Well, you can! You'll need two things: your Heartbreak Wisdom Journal and about ninety seconds.

The next time you feel an emotion that you just want to run from, grab your journal, turn to an empty page, and make two columns. In fact, you may want to draw the columns and questions in your journal now so you don't have to look for this section when you're also trying to run from that emotion. In the left-hand column, quickly write down the one to three thoughts that are bothering you the most. For example, you might include things such as, "I'll never, ever find love again," or "It's all my fault," or "There is something so wrong with me that I always choose the wrong guy." In the second column, list as quickly as you can where these emotions live in your body. If you pay attention, you see that every feeling has an accompanying bodily sensation. It may be as simple as "Adrenaline flooding my stomach" or as particular as "My right shoulder blade suddenly feels pinned to my spine." Be specific. Be creative. The moment you arrive at the correct physical analogy for your difficult emotion, turn all your attention to the sensation, not the thought that provoked it. Don't try to dispel it but, instead, relax with it by turning your attention to it.

Paying attention is synonymous with offering loving-kindness. As Zen teacher and poet John Tarrant says, "Attention is the most basic form of love. Through it we bless and are blessed."

Gradually your physical sensation will begin to shift, lessen, and, perhaps, fade away. In this way, you allow the sensation to be what it is and play itself out by relaxing with it.

7

Yes, You Have Lost Your Mind (But It's Okay)

IN HEARTBREAK, the first thing you may notice is that you have lost your mind. Seriously. What else would you call it? You can't control your thoughts. Your ability to say, "Not now," to the mental and emotional onslaught is approximately zilch. You're in a business meeting and you feel compelled to share your feelings, something you'd as soon have done before the breakup as show up in a negligee. You're watching your favorite program that always makes you laugh, but this time Elaine's lipstick reminds you of the shade you wore on your first date and you dissolve into tears. (Not that there's anything wrong with that.) You want to sleep, but grief continues to disturb your peace, even after you've fallen asleep. It seems there is nothing you can do about it.

My friend Laura called me a few days after she had chosen to break up with her boyfriend, having concluded that he would never welcome her into his life as she wished. Even though they had gone on many fun dates and hung out a lot, he had always kept her at arm's length. He was uninterested in her emotional life and failed to show up for her—physically and emotionally—during crises. After a year of hoping he would change, she realized that he would never offer her the kind of closeness, friendship, and intimacy she desired in a life partner. So even though she loved him, she got up the courage to end it, and did. But she was devastated.

From the way the relationship had started, she had no reason to expect this outcome. When they first fell in love, she had felt sure that he was the one. They had been professionally acquainted for five years and always had a bit of a crush on each other. When he heard that her previous relationship was over, he began to court her via the telephone and sexy emails. He lived in Dallas, she in Austin. The three-hour drive and work commitments kept them from getting together face-to-face for a few weeks after it was clear that they would, but, as can happen so easily in courtship conducted in the airwaves, those weeks were pure delight and romance. She would receive emails from him throughout the day, just checking in, telling little jokes, reminding her how beautiful she was. At night, they spoke on the phone until two or three in the morning.

When they finally did get together for a weekend, the romance came down to earth with a perfect landing. They didn't immediately rip each other's clothes off and jump into bed, much as they wanted to. They allowed the romantic tension to build. They went out for a long, leisurely dinner where their desire for each other played as a delicious secret against the backdrop of restaurant noise and commotion. Then they went for a long walk, the sense of magical connection growing stronger with each mundane scene they passed: A couple walking their dog. The line at the movie theater on the corner. A car parallel parking in front of the bookstore. Every commonplace occurrence they witnessed heightened the sense of mystery and attraction to each other. The weekend was as intense and gratifying as she could have hoped.

I could tell by her voice when she told me about their time together that she had been transported from the ground of workaday existence to the space of mystical, sexual, emotional connection with another. I was so happy for her. And I was also scared. Yes, they were grown-ups. Yes, they had both had enough experience in relationships to know how to avoid the obvious pitfalls. Yes, they had discussed the portent of beginning a relationship—but no matter how cool you are, this kind of connection unleashes heat and powerful energies. And it takes a lot of heart and wisdom to manage them. Still, she had been very clear that she was looking for a life partner, nothing short of someone with whom to make a life together. Period. And he agreed—this was also what he sought.

So their relationship began. The nightly phone calls continued, and they tried to spend every weekend together, during which time they discussed ways to merge their lives more completely. Could she continue to do her job from his home or would she have to quit? If so, would it make more sense for him to quit his job and move in with her? Or could they find a home somewhere in the middle, halfway between each of their places of employment?

After several months, trouble began to brew. Yes, they loved each other. Sex was still great. Conversations were still deep. But she became unnerved by what she thought was an increasing emotional distance. He started to tell her little things about herself that he did not like. She wasn't neat enough, a bit too frivolous with money. He became finicky about how much time he would allocate to spend with her and indicated he might require more privacy and personal space than she did—perhaps they shouldn't spend every weekend together. *Okay,* she thought. *He's very introspective and has two kids, and I respect his need for space. And he's right—I could stand to be tidier and more careful with money.* She reviewed ways she might change to better her life *and* please him.

But her motivation to please him dissolved when she tripped at work and broke her ankle, and he opted not to make the drive to take care of her because he was too busy with work. *What the hell kind of boyfriend is this,* she thought. *If he only wants to hang out when I'm at my best, then he's probably not a great candidate for growing old together.*

When the one you love does not *choose* you on the deepest level, although he may actually love you in his own (bizarre) way, the pain of not being chosen is too much to bear. In a great show of self-respect and personal dignity, she elected to end it rather than tolerate being less than fully embraced.

But the cost was high. She lost her mind. Not in the crazy-kooky sense, but in the way we all do when our hearts are broken. She could no longer choose what to think about. No matter how many obstacles she tried to throw in its path, the heartbreak train steamrolled over everything. This is how it works. No matter how hard you try by throwing yourself into work, watching *Law & Order* marathons, getting drunk, or getting drastic haircuts, insistent thoughts about this loss trump everything. Maybe these things could distract you for a few minutes, but eventually the mind returns to rehashing detail after detail of the hows, whys, and what the hells of the breakup. Even during sleep, your brain spews image after nightmarish image of pain and sorrow and rage. Your mind is gone. You have lost authority. You are no longer mistress of your domain.

Quite reasonably, you try to reassert dominion. In addition to the aforementioned examples, you might try to do anything you can to restart the relationship, under any terms. The grief-stricken soul can come up with some pretty wacky justifications for why it's a good idea to get with someone who doesn't love you quite enough. Or you could make an airtight case for why he's a complete asshole in an effort to drum up sufficient outrage and resentment to drown out the sorrow. You could give up and just lie around numbly, cookie crumbs strewn about and Kleenex bits stuck to your nose. It's tempting to try to do anything at all to induce a sensation that is momentarily stronger than the wail of your broken heart.

Unfortunately, none of these things works. Instead, they whip you up into an even greater frenzy because, instead of disappearing, the banished thoughts return with double intensity. All the explanations, strategies, and emotional displays in the world cannot distract you from what has happened: you have had your heart broken. The sorrow is profound and cannot and will not be subsumed in any other sensation. You have hit the bottom. Okay, at least now you know where you are.

Job number one when it comes to a broken heart is regaining your mind. This is exactly what the practice of meditation teaches. It trains the mind to be your ally, not your foe. In meditation, you simply stop struggling with yourself. Instead, you allow your attention to ride the breath (detailed instructions to follow), and every time a thought arises, you neither embrace it nor repel it. You don't feel gratitude for good thoughts or dismay at bad ones. You simply notice each thought with a nonjudgmental "thank you very much" and go back to the naturalness and honesty of the breath. In my tradition, we describe this relationship to thoughts as "touch and go." You neither pull a thought toward you nor do you push it away. You simply notice your thoughts, touch them lightly with your attention, and then—and this is an operative word—*gently* let them go. Through repeatedly returning to the simplicity of the breath, you cultivate steadiness of attention, the ability to maintain focus on an object of your choosing. You have some say over what to pay attention to and what to ignore.

A person who can place her awareness where she likes is a formidable creature indeed. Most often our attention is a bit of a tart, hooking up with whatever thought shows up first or waves the brightest trinkets. You may fully intend to do one thing with your mind while it has another idea altogether, like when you want to clean out your email inbox and it wants to surf around for new shoes. And forget about it when you're trying to get over a breakup. Your own mind turns on you. You want to sleep, but you can't stop thinking about him. You want to think about how you got into this situation, but instead you fall asleep. You command yourself to pay attention to work, but can't because you hear his favorite song and fall apart. You tell yourself you want to do your homework, but instead write him a thirty-page letter about what a jerk he is and how much you still love him.

You need to regain some control here, but not in an angry, willful way. Instead of fighting the pain, extend to it the hand of friendship. Think of your heartache as a profoundly upset child, a baby, whom you love very, very much. When your baby wakes up screaming and sobbing, you don't walk into her room and say, "See here. This is ridiculous. Buck up already." Or, "Well, it's your own fault. I told you not to sleep on your stomach." Nor do you attempt to dissect the plotline and meaning of her distress; babies don't know and don't care. It's also not a good idea to try to drown her out or distract her by telling her about *your* worst nightmare, throwing some toys in the crib, or turning up the music so that you can no longer hear her. All you can do is approach with kindness, pick her up in your arms, and remain with her until the last teardrop falls. You willingly bring all your attention to her (babies can tell when you don't really want to be there) and then simply *stay*. Supreme gentleness is called for; anything else causes the emotional agitation to escalate.

The practice of meditation is just this: approaching yourself exactly as you are, witnessing yourself with kindness (not judgment), and staying by your own side for as long as it takes. Just as with a crying baby, when it comes to your heart, simply accept it as it is, and it immediately begins to pacify. You will feel incredible relief when you simply stop struggling against your pain. Huge.

The practice of meditation is the most direct way to do this because instead of categorizing and managing emotion, it teaches you how to turn *toward* what is occurring and experience it. You can begin to know and understand yourself honestly. This act of allowing, although so simple, is also quite precious. It creates something called volatility, an active state of change. For instance, when heated, water becomes volatile and turns to vapor. In its volatile state, it more easily combines with other substances; it's able to change.

Like it or not, you have been entered into a state of sacred volatility. Whatever you thought you possessed—love, security, a picture of the future, a sense of being lovable—is shaken loose from its appearance, rendered momentarily formless through the fire of heartbreak. Now, depending on your approach, you can attempt to squelch this process and retain possession of whatever old beliefs you have left—or, through the grace of your attention and acceptance, you can open the door wide, let some air in, and watch the flames grow. Let them burn until they burn out. By doing this, you let them make room for something new to rise out of the ashes.

Through the power of meditation you establish yourself in the groundless nature of heartbreak, no matter how paradoxical that sounds. You develop tolerance for uncertainty and, as you are able to do so, the discomfort of simply not knowing what is happening to you or why or where it will all end up transforms your heartbreak into wisdom. The gateway to wisdom is not-knowing. If you already think you know, nothing new can enter. By establishing yourself in uncertainty, your heart essence refines itself into what it already is, just beneath the surface of agitation: a kind of love that is simply indestructible.

In this way heartbreak itself becomes a most profound and uncompromising teacher.

8

How to Meditate

MEDITATION CREATES the conditions for transforming pain into wisdom. It can quell the 24/7 antics of a freaked-out mind. The very first job you have for your broken heart is to re-assert some dominion over your thoughts. Meditation cultivates tranquility, joy, vitality, and love, and helps you work with difficult emotions such as terror, rage, and despair. By cultivation, I mean it creates inner transformation that gives rise to your own, god-given, birthright-grade qualities of inner peace and relaxation. These things are *still there inside you*. (They really, really are.) And sitting meditation is the foundational practice that reawakens these qualities. Far more than a stress-reduction technique, meditation is the ground of peace and joy.

I'm going to teach you a meditation practice called the "Practice of Tranquility," which may seem completely impossible right now—but it isn't. Tranquility is not something that descends on you when you're able to get the circumstances just right: perfect job, perfect house, perfect relationship, perfect weight. Tranquility is your natural mind state—it is the state to which you were born, and the mind knows how to return there if you just allow it. No matter how shaken up you are, within you is the knowledge of how, very naturally, to return to balance.

When a newborn baby bursts into tears, he doesn't look very tranquil. But at some point the storm passes and the tranquil state is reestablished. There is no residue. The baby who was red-faced and squealing moments ago is now smiling and playing peacefully in his crib. This isn't a trick. The baby isn't rationalizing away his pain or pretending to be over it so you won't worry about him. The upset is simply gone and his mind returns whence it came: peace. Your mind can do this, too, and the Practice of Tranquility can show you how.

This practice is ancient—over 2,500 years old—and although it is associated with Buddhism, there is nothing particularly religious about it. It is simply the practice of resting your awareness on your breath and, every time your attention strays, bringing it back to your breath.

Your mind already knows how to meditate. It is always resting on something—most often, however, on thoughts based in hope or fear, the past or the future. When you begin to notice your thinking, you'll see that it is rarely focused on the present. Even if you try to stay in the present, you find that you keep slipping into some kind of worry or expectation or judgment. The mind is always commenting on something. In meditation, you practice consciously placing your attention on an object of your choosing instead of allowing it to gallop all over creation. It is not an easy practice necessarily, but it is a very simple one and you don't need to adopt any foreign point of view or belief system. I'm going to give you detailed instructions below, and if you wish, you can visit my website for guided audio instruction at susanpiver.com/meditation _instruction.

Meditation is the noble act of making friends with yourself, just as you are. This is the very first and, arguably, most important step you can take to restore your heart to balance. When you sit and meditate, you are agreeing to hang out with yourself, exactly as you are.

Instructions for the Practice of Tranquility

Find a comfortable place to sit. If you can sit on a meditation cushion, that's great. If this is too uncomfortable for any reason, it's fine to sit on a chair.

It's helpful to designate a particular spot for meditation, so, if possible, choose a particular room or corner of a room to establish your practice. Make your sitting area pleasant. If you wish, you could sit in front of a shelf or table with some cherished or beautiful objects on them, like fresh flowers, some river stones, or a picture of someone or something you love. Keep it simple. The idea is to create a spot that you feel good about returning to. For pictures of how different people arrange their sitting areas, please visit my website at susanpiver.com/meditation_resources.

There are three aspects to pay attention to in meditation practice.

Body

The practice begins with how you take your seat. The main thing to remember is to sit up straight, not rigidly, but in a relaxed, upright position. I like to use the analogy of a tree, whose roots are planted in the ground but that also sways and moves with the wind. Your posture should be firmly planted but also supple. Feel your sit-bones reach down into the earth and the crown of your head reach slightly up, as if some kind and gentle person had put his palm a few centimeters above it and you would like to touch it. When you sit upright like this, you are proclaiming your dignity.

If you are seated on a cushion, cross your legs loosely in front of you. Some people prefer to have their knees lower than the hips, some higher. Play around and see which works for you. Some people feel most comfortable with only a very thin cushion to elevate their hips; others require a cushion that is one or two feet high. You may have to experiment with cushion heights to find the right setup for yourself.

If you are on a chair, scoot forward so that your back is not resting on anything and your feet are flat on the floor. For most people who meditate sitting in a chair, it's nice to have the knees a little higher than your hips. To accomplish this, you may need to put a cushion under your feet. (You can see my website, susanpiver.com/meditation_resources, for varieties of cushions and photos of different people sitting in the way that is comfortable for them. Everyone is different.)

When you've found a comfortable posture, place your hands, palms down, just above your knees or at midthigh. Let your shoulders and belly relax.

Tuck your chin a little bit to bring some length to the back of the neck. Your mouth should be closed with the lips slightly parted, tongue resting on the roof of the mouth. Let the jaw relax.

In this practice, your eyes remain open. Your gaze is soft and cast slightly down, to a spot about six to eight feet in front of you. It's not like you're staring at that spot or at anything in particular, more like vision is streaming out from your eyes and mixing with space instead of targeting anything in particular. Although they are open, your eyes are relaxed with the sense that they are sitting back in their sockets as opposed to straining forward, which is how it usually feels. It doesn't matter what your gaze comes to rest on, just let it settle on a spot six to eight feet in front.

Breath

Once you have established your posture (which is the most complicated part!), begin to notice the rise and fall of your breath, in and out through the nose. Each breath is different. Can you tell how? There is no need to breathe in any particular way, just allow attention to ride the breath like waves in the ocean.

Placing awareness on the breath is different from thinking about the breath. Here is a simple demonstration of what I mean by placement of attention. Without moving or looking, right now allow your awareness to settle around your right big toe. Allow yourself to simply become conscious of that little piggy. Notice if it feels squished or snug in your sock, or if you can feel the air around it. Now, also without moving or looking, move your awareness to your left earlobe. Again, just notice it hanging out there in space.

Maybe it's adorned with an earring; perhaps it's covered by your hair. Now move awareness back to the right big toe.

Whatever just moved is your *attention,* and that is what you place on your breath. So go ahead and do that, with a light touch.

Mind

At some point you may notice that your attention has drifted away from your breath and become absorbed in thought. That is absolutely no problem, none whatsoever. I have heard people say such things as, "I tried to meditate but I couldn't stop thinking! There's no way I can do it." Well, of course you can't. Trying to stop thinking is like telling your nose not to smell anything. It can't help it; that's just what a nose does. This is what trying not to think is like. So instead of trying not to think, in meditation you develop a different relationship to your thoughts. When thoughts arise, you simply notice them and allow them to float by. Keep your attention on your breath. When a particular thought absconds with your attention, as soon as you notice this, just return *your attention to your breath.* It doesn't matter how long you've been "gone." The important thing is to come back. Gently let the thought ease away like a wave recedes back into the ocean. It doesn't matter how wonderful, horrendous, boring, creative, or critically insightful your thought has been . . . just let go.

When it comes to thoughts, instead of becoming absorbed in them, notice them as you would clouds in the sky. Just like clouds, some thoughts are cheerful and bright while some seem to bear ominous portent. Some are fat and fluffy and beautiful, and others are barely perceptible beyond a far-off streak of white. Sometimes clouds block the sky altogether, but you know that just beyond them, the sun is always shining, clear and bright. Meditation researcher and practitioner Jon Kabat-Zinn says that in meditation practice, instead of identifying with the clouds, we identify ourselves as the sky. The sky doesn't care what kind of clouds pass through or how long they stay. And, just like the sky, we can hold it all and know that no matter what direction we happen to be facing, somewhere it is always east and somewhere the sun is always rising.

When you have established your body, breath, and mind in the practice of meditation, try to sit for around ten minutes per day. It's better to sit for a short period every day than a longer period on some days. Consistency is more important than duration.

Most people like to sit in the morning, but you may be a night owl and prefer to sit when you get home in the evening. The best time to practice is the time that you will stick with, so choose a particular time slot and try to make it a routine.

At some point you may feel like increasing your meditation time and, please, go ahead and do so. Just don't make it a race or try to prove anything to yourself. Take it very slowly. A good plan is to try ten minutes a day for a month. At the end of that month, decide whether you want to continue with ten-minute sessions, stop altogether, or increase the time. If you want to increase, do so by small increments, say, five minutes. Then, after a month of sitting for fifteen minutes, you can make a decision about where to go from there.

I want to mention something extremely important at this point, so listen up. If you find that you want to make meditation an ongoing part of your life, please find a meditation instructor. Working with your own mind can seem like trying to get your eyeball to look at itself and can get very odd and confusing. It's vital to find someone who has been practicing for longer than you and who can offer you practical guidance. In the Shambhala tradition, people are trained to be meditation instructors, just as I have been, and the service is free; all you have to do is show up at a local center and request one. You could also visit your local Zen or Vipassana center and find support there. The only important thing is to go somewhere credible, meaning a place that is affiliated with a lineage that has been around for, say, several thousand years. Stay away from new age nonsense. (See appendix C for a list of meditation resources, including meditation centers.)

WHEN YOU HAVE suffered a loss, the contents of your heart are like the sparkles inside a snow globe. All day long your thoughts shake the globe furiously and the little flakes swirl and swirl. The only way to settle the situation is not by willing the flakes to settle or looking away and hoping that when you look back, things will have changed—but simply to put the globe down. Meditation creates the stable surface on which the mind can rest. It will then settle on its own. Watch while, one by one, each flake slowly drifts to the surface and melts away until all that is left is clarity and stillness and you can now see exactly where you are.

The Indian philosopher J. Krishnamurti said, "When you begin to notice what you are without trying to change it, what you are begins to undergo transformation." Through the simple act of noticing, you will transform heartbreak into wisdom.

9

If You Accept Pain,
It Cannot Hurt You

THE MOST HELPFUL THING you can do when you feel upset is basically the opposite of what everyone tells you to do. Why doesn't anyone tell you that leaning into what terrifies you is far more effective (and interesting) than doing everything in your power to escape it? However, in moving toward what frightens you, you may find that your fear is not what you thought it was.

The early-twentieth-century psychoanalyst Karen Horney described three neurotic responses to anxiety: some people, she said, move against the source of stress (aggression), while others move away from it (withdrawal), while the third group moves toward it (compliance). But there is a fourth option: simply leaning into emotion as you would lean into a strong breeze. Not to move against, not to move away, and not to try to pacify, but simply to experience it.

When my friend Heather had her heart broken, she embarked on a rigorous period of self-examination. Some aspects of her quest proved quite helpful, such as examining childhood wounds that could have contributed to her choice of an unsuitable partner. Again. But other aspects didn't seem so useful. She became convinced that she had "attracted" Tom because of unfinished emotional business from her past and that, once she resolved it, she would attract the right partner. Heather began working night and day to isolate her old wounds in order to rid herself of them for good and, in this way, to avoid having her heart broken ever again. She determined to devote all her resources to this task.

One night she simply found herself at the end of her rope. It was almost four o'clock in the morning and she was sitting on her sofa, surrounded by earmarked self-help and psychology books, dozens of journals in which she had kept track of her self-investigations, and a nearly empty bottle of wine. Although she had learned a lot during this time about her wounds from her family of origin and what circumstances in particular were likely to trigger her, she had made almost no progress in actually *feeling* better. It had been sixteen months since the breakup and she felt only a tiny bit less raw and awkward and devastated than she did the day it happened. How long, she wondered, before she felt some of the burden of sorrow lifted from her shoulders? How long would she have to feel these feelings? She felt as if she were fighting for her life.

Maybe it was the late hour and maybe it was the wine, but suddenly she became completely sick of having a broken heart. She swept all the books and journals off the coffee table and onto the floor and burst into tears. *Come on,* she thought. *I give up. I'm tired of fighting. If this is going to kill me, kill me already.* She lay down on the couch, closed her eyes, and waited for who knows what.

And then the strangest thing happened. She had an image of a dam filled to bursting and herself running from end to end, trying to stuff flimsy bits of tissue into each hole that opened up. Every time she plugged one up, it burst again within moments. No matter how fast she ran, she could not stop the impending flood. So she just stopped trying and the dam broke. Heather fully expected to be drowned. In this half-dream state, she watched the waves wash over her time and again. But instead of drowning, she found herself swimming in them, frantically at first, and then playfully, like a kid at the beach. She started to laugh.

On the spot, Heather realized that, in large part, the effort to plumb her psychological depths was really an attempt to stave off the flow of emotion, but instead of helping, it had exhausted her. When she realized this, once again she burst into tears. This time they weren't tears of frustration and agitation, however, but because she felt sad for herself. She saw that in all this self-study she had actually been ignoring herself. Then, like a mom holding her baby, she let the feelings come and sat with herself as she cried. Eventually she fell asleep and, when she woke up a few hours later, although all her problems weren't solved, she had a sense of calm and self-respect. She had leaned into her feelings. She had taken ownership of her heart, not as a nurse in a psych ward, but as a friend.

Of course, the broken heart searches intensely for meaning. We are drawn to dissecting the situation in order to learn about it. Pain this deep must mean something. However, while it is good to seek to understand what may be going on beneath the surface to explain how life could flip-flop from being something basically manageable to a hellish experience, it is very tricky. When searching for explanations, you can easily move too fast, to settle on the first thing you come upon that happens to make sense in the moment. What makes sense one day (I'm too needy) has no validity the next (I'm not needy! He was incapable of love!). As your emotions roil, moving unpredictably between despair, outrage, astonishment, and intense weariness, possible explanations shift as well. When you're despairing, you may search your psychological history for the moment that gave rise to the personality flaws that now make you basically unlovable. But when you're furious, the idea of such flaws seems ridiculous and, instead, you dissect his behavior for the reasons you broke up. When you're simply reeling from shock, it could lead you to question the decisions you've made in life that got you to this situation in the first place, in an effort never to make those mistakes again. And when you're plumb worn out, the only explanation that makes sense is "Life sucks." You simply don't have the energy to come up with anything better. These explanations roll and tumble without end, taking you with them.

Even though there may indeed be validity in each explanation you arrive at (you probably do have some icky flaws, he probably does, too, perhaps you have made some bad decisions, and, of course, sometimes life *does* suck), somehow that validity does nothing to make you feel better. Arriving at any of these conclusions does nothing to help with your suffering. In fact, conclusions may increase your suffering, no matter how psychologically or philosophically acute. This is because the only thing that really helps emotions is to shine the gentle light of awareness on them, get to know them as sad and lonely friends, and hold them to you for comfort. As the American Buddhist Pema Chödrön counsels, it is best to "feel the feelings and drop the story."

The Practice of Tranquility meditation teaches you exactly how to release your mind, thought by thought. Hopefully you've begun to experiment with it enough to have a sense of how good it feels to rest your mind.

TRY THIS
Flashes of Meditation

THE EXERCISE I'm about to describe to you may sound impossibly simple, but it is actually quite profound. I call it "flashing on the mind of meditation." What this means is that, instead of meditating (because you're driving, say, or on deadline for your master's thesis), you simply *remember* what it's like to meditate. For example, if I asked you right now, "What does it feel like to meditate?" what happens? To answer the question, your mind momentarily resettles itself in the "posture" of meditation and in this way you get a tiny hit, or flash, of the meditation. Repeatedly flashing on the mind of meditation (which takes less

than a second) is the next best thing to a formal practice session, and it interrupts a train of thought before
it can run away with you altogether.

The quest for self-improvement (to fix everything
that's wrong with you so that you never get your heart
broken again) can actually block you from achieving
emotional balance. The effort to gather, tag, and reha-
bilitate your flaws can become an act of aggression,
even hatred, toward yourself. The antidote is provided
by The Practice of Tranquility, which teaches self-
acceptance without judgment or agenda. In the end,
this, more than any self-help strategy, is the key to
healing.

10

Sex Might Help

WHEN I WAS TRYING to get over my own dreadful heart-break, what set me on the road to recovery was spending the weekend in bed with someone I hardly knew. Yes, I know this isn't the typical recommendation (and I'm not recommending it, I swear) but out of all the help I got from relationship books, therapy sessions, and personal affirmations ("I am loved, loving, and lovable . . .") what actually began to turn my situation around was sex with this guy I sort of knew who lived in California. I mean, I knew him (we were colleagues), but we weren't friends.

However, we had had a friendly flirtation at business conferences, and when he found out my relationship was over, he invited me to get on a plane and meet him for a weekend in the hills surrounding Santa Fe. All my girlfriends were dead set against this. They told me I was acting crazy, that this was a very bad idea. They warned me against the rebound relationship. They reminded me that we lived halfway across the country from each other and I had never spent more than sixty consecutive minutes with him. They worried that I would come back in much worse shape than when I left. Ha! As if that were possible. I was not in my right mind, it was true, and if what I needed was a relationship, all their dire predictions may have come true. But it wasn't. What I needed, it turned out, was a love affair.

I boarded the plane for Santa Fe with the feeling of a kamikaze pilot about to dive-bomb her own heartache and return either triumphant or in a body bag. Whatever. At this point I really didn't care. The guy I was going to meet was tall and cute, creative and funny, and most important, I found, had a quality that could prevent a weekend of this sort from turning into emotional S&M: sweetness. He was just a nice guy. He had the sort of kindness that you can sense a mile off. Luckily for me, he was also organized and efficient. After he gathered that I could barely tie my shoes let alone make decisions about a weekend away, he booked our hotel, made dinner reservations, and figured out a bunch of cool places we could visit. So I went.

He waited for me at the airport and we shared a taxi to our hotel, suddenly nervous and uncertain about what we were doing, or why. Nonetheless, all nerves fell away as soon as we checked into our lovely room, as did all plans to hike, sightsee, or dine out. There was no courtship; we went straight to naked. We stayed in bed for three days and I guess we must have ordered room service for sustenance; I have no memory of food. I only remember closing my eyes, taking a deep breath and letting myself love him, and he me. I really, really gave him my love.

But by "love" I don't mean falling in love. I wasn't all "He is so cute, so funny, so smart; I want to make him mine." Nope. I just let all the feelings of love and longing and sadness and tenderness that were already in my heart rise up to the surface and find expression in the way I looked at him, held him, needed him, took joy in him. It felt so agenda-less, so liberating. I didn't spend time wondering if this was a safe person to entrust my heart to; I just gave him my heart. I didn't spend time wondering what I felt about him; I just allowed my feelings to show, moment to moment. I don't recall thinking one thought about the future of our relationship. We made love and slept and made love, and a few times I just lay there and cried. He didn't try to comfort me nor did he ignore me; he just sweetly hung out with me until I stopped.

When the weekend was over, we went home and I don't think

I ever saw him again. We may have spoken on the phone once or twice, and my recollection is that we made halfhearted attempts to get together again. But I think we both knew that what happened between us wasn't the start of a relationship. It was a love affair. And, whether because we were smart or scared, we simply let the experience slide away.

Okay, so I lucked out. Neither of us had diseases of mind or body, neither of us had ulterior motives, and nobody ended up drunk dialing at 3:00 a.m. If I ran into him now, I would express my enduring gratitude. I would thank him for helping me remember that I was lovable and sexy. I'd tell him that he gave me the courage to face my broken heart instead of trying to run away from it. I'd want him to know that our weekend together showed me just how alive and strong my heart really was, how easily I could still love, and how powerfully. The whole thing was a giant blessing and, in my experience before and since, not the way these things tend to turn out. So, phew.

Although it's very tricky, I learned that a love affair could work out even if you're not superyoung or from France, and that love affairs and relationships are actually two different things. It just so happens that we expect our intimate relationships to be both and, if you're very lucky, one day you'll find one that is. In the meantime, though, here are some things to remember about love affairs: they live and die on kindness; both parties have to be willing to give their hearts completely and then let go; and, most important, love really, truly does heal all.

11

Have Faith

THERE IS A WAY to have faith, to trust, even when you have
been betrayed. I don't mean that you should cultivate faith in any
particular deity or concept if you don't already have that. You can
have faith in your own experience exactly as it is. You can come to
know it as your unfailing and perfect teacher.

Each moment is an opportunity to cultivate openness, joy, and
authenticity. With the Practice of Tranquility as your working
basis or default setting, you are able to slow down in the midst of
daily experience and choose your actions and reactions more skillfully. When sorrow rises, you can turn to it, taste it, and wait for it
to dissolve. This way you learn not to fear your own sorrow. When
an irritating coworker asks you *again* how to change the toner in
the printer, you can catch yourself before you snap at her and simply get up, walk her to the device, and carefully teach her how it is
done. You can make this tiny moment into an opportunity to cultivate kindness. Even simple, everyday tasks like grocery shopping,
filling the car with gas, or walking the dog can become an exercise
in mindfulness if you just slow down and pay attention to what
you're doing. In this way, every moment of every day has something
to teach you—the right thing, the very thing you need to learn.
Looked at this way, as the American Buddhist teacher Tsultrim

Allione says, "Faith is a form of relaxation," because you can stop trying too hard and just wait for life to bring you its lessons.

This definition of faith is quite different from becoming convinced of the truth of a particular point of view and then sticking with it. Holding tight. Feeding whatever arises in your life through the faith machine in order to come out with the "right" answer at the other end. Personally, I would be ecstatic if this were all it took to make life make sense. But faith is not suspending your reason or judgment. It's not deciding that you believe in something or someone outside of yourself. Faith is a kind of supreme openness. An absolute faith closes the door to possibilities—one glance at the day's headlines will show you what this'll get you.

I mean, think about it. It's an act of faith to go into the events of your life not knowing what they all mean. It's an act of faith to allow things to unfold and unfold and unfold, and to be willing to include in your life not just what makes you feel happy, but also your agitation, confusion, doubt, and personal displays of ridiculousness without drawing harsh conclusions. Actually, faith begins to look a lot like fearlessness. It looks a lot like genuine confidence. I once thought that confidence meant feeling certain I would never appear ridiculous again. Au contraire. It means that even when you feel ridiculous—or devastated or sleepy or impassioned—you can relax about it. Even when you're completely anxious, you can relax about that, too.

Faith begins with testing out the idea that the events of your life may not be for you or against you. I realize that may sound funny. How can the things that make you feel good not be beneficial and those that hurt you not be bad for you? Well, conventionally speaking, perhaps they are. Perhaps what builds you up leads to your betterment and what injures you tears you down. But maybe not. Maybe all of it is simply your experience in the moment, and it's not how many good experiences you can link together that build the bridge to happiness, but how many *genuine* ones you can have. How truly can you be in your own life? How sharply can you feel your own joy and how deeply can you experience your sorrows? This is what seems to lead to happiness, not chasing after good experiences and strategizing away bad ones.

You learn how to stabilize yourself in a state of openness through practicing meditation. Then something funny starts to happen. You become aware, tentatively at first, but with more and more certainty as you develop trust, that your life is leading somewhere. A mysterious sort of congruence between your inner experience and your external circumstances begins to develop. You may start to notice synchronicities and auspicious coincidences, chance ideas, meetings, or events that seem to harmonize with your state of mind. You can't force these things to happen, nor can you look too hard for them. The more you relax, the more they arise. This arising lies at the heart of faith. For me, the more I practice and the more I risk opening myself to even my most painful feelings, the more wind I find at my back helping me out of difficulties and into balance. I've come to see that my life has a life of its own. Instead of trying to commandeer it, I'm trying to follow it.

In this sense, faith is not so much a belief that everything is somehow going to work out for the best, which can be very, very difficult to imagine when your heart is broken, when you are desperate to believe that you're feeling some kind of divine redirection away from what was bad for you and toward what is going to be way better than you ever imagined. This isn't really a good state of mind to walk around in. First, it presumes that you know what's best for you and, honestly, I've never found evidence that this is a big enough point of view.

A lot of people believe that by thinking positively and expecting good things to happen, you can make good things happen. Recently I spoke to my friend Stephen Mitchell, an internationally respected translator of the world's great wisdom texts, including the *Tao Te Ching,* the Bhagavad Gita, and the book of Job, about this subject. I asked if in his lifelong study of the core teachings of all religions, he'd ever come across that idea. I wrote down what he said because it was so excellent. Here it is:

> The teaching of every one of the great sacred texts is that control is an illusion. When you understand that ultimately you are not the doer, you can step back from yourself. That is the only path to serenity. In other words,

letting go of the illusion of control, and realizing that you never had control in the first place, allows you to live in the most dazzlingly intelligent, beautiful, and kind reality that you could ever have imagined—and beyond what you could have imagined.

I don't know about you, but I'll have what he's having. When I thought about it, I realized that all the many things I had longed for throughout my life and had been lucky enough to get—like a good relationship, great friends, and a cool job—hadn't exactly made me into Mahatma Gandhi. In a lot of ways I was just as riled up and dissatisfied as ever. So maybe I wasn't the supreme arbiter of all things good for me. Now what? According to Stephen Mitchell, actually, all I had to do was relax, to allow the world to dazzle me instead of the other way around. So I'm trying.

When I can relax enough, I see that, just like me, everyone—regular people, great superstars, and profound sages—probably all started out worrying that the world was going to eat them alive or that they simply weren't lovable enough. We are all just looking for some kind of happiness. Sometimes things work out for us, and sometimes they don't. It really doesn't matter. Eventually all our hopes and fears are going to dissolve, and at the end of our lives, according to all the deathbed reports we've ever received, the only thing that will matter is how loving and brave we've been.

All those dying people can't be wrong when they say that all the things you want and all the things you dread are just like waves in the ocean. Eventually they just become reabsorbed into the vast play of the sea. And you know what? The ocean doesn't care. It never gives up. It can accommodate it all, gentle waves that lap the shore and those that roil up ferociously, tiny tidal pools and great, freezing depths. The real secret, the great ones say, is that we are much more like the ocean than the waves. Underneath all our hopes and fears is profound stillness and the memory of how to return to it.

Part
Two

See Where You Are

12

Betrayal Stands Alone

Betrayal, of all the woundings that may be suffered by the soul, can be the greatest agent of the sacred. This wound has always had an awful and luminous quality surrounding it. It marks the end of primal, unconscious trust, and forces upon us those terrible conditions that accompany the taking of the next step. . . . The condition of this trust has been a subtle and powerful binding that blocks the fullness of the greater consciousness needed to respond to new situations—situations that cannot be met within the old conditions.

—Jean Houston, *The Search for the Beloved*

ON ONE TYPICAL post-breakup day, I was lying on the couch, staring into space, not watching whatever was on TV, wearing my fat sweatpants and an inside-out long-sleeved T-shirt with half-used Kleenex tissues stuffed up the sleeves. It was two o'clock on a sunny Thursday afternoon, but I simply couldn't bring myself to do anything but sink lower and lower into a dark pit of horrible imaginings. Him with her. Me alone. A bitter, loveless future consisting of postmenopausal activities such as comparing early-bird specials and shopping for pants with elastic waistbands.

On the coffee table were a hundred self-help books and highlighter pens in every shade of the rainbow. I picked one book at random; it was titled *The Search for the Beloved* by Jean Houston, and, by grace, flipped open to the page containing the quote above. My heart, which I had thought was dead, stopped. *Of course.* I had been betrayed. My ex-boyfriend had reneged on his promise to love me, and this odious event had a name. *Betrayal.* Somehow, knowing this calmed me down, and I began to contemplate betrayal. My conclusion: it *is* the most difficult of all woundings.

Betrayal comes in many forms—it's not just about being cheated on or left for another. It's about any promise, overt or implied, that has been broken without your participation in the decision, or even knowing that a decision was on the table. It's about believing something that you later find out is untrue. It's no wonder that the first response to betrayal is likely to be denial. It's an enormous shock to find out that a solid reality is not so solid after all. It can feel like the most deviant form of attack.

When betrayal is at the root of your pain, something horrible is unleashed, different (and perhaps more horrible) than the pain of disappointment, grief, or anger. With other causes of suffering, you can at least pretend you have some measure of control. You can blame the other person for disappointing you. You can read books that outline and predict the course of grief. And when you're angry, you can always fall back on self-righteousness.

But when you are betrayed, you have been blindsided, and your vulnerability is confirmed. You lose a misplaced innocence that you can never regain. Your ability to trust is basically obliterated—and not just your trust in your own perceptions and your trust in the person you loved. Once you lose trust in one person, your trust in all beings is undermined, making the future seem like a giant land mine. It makes sense that you'd try to take refuge in religion, new-agey explanations, workaholism, extreme cynicism, and/or outrageous haircuts. It makes sense that you'd write off the entire male sex, certain ethnicities, and various professions. (I once had a friend who swore never to date another Latino mandolin player.) It seems that nothing good can come of betrayal. But this assumption is wrong.

To recognize the wisdom that underlies your betrayal may take some time. The effect of betrayal is no small thing, and recovering from it requires a reordering in your brain of how reality works. I think this is what Houston meant when she wrote that betrayal "forces upon us those terrible conditions that accompany the taking of the next step."

It is at this exact juncture that we separate the girls from the women. A girl attempts to soothe herself by taking potshots at others—"All guys suck"—and mocking her own need to love and trust others. A woman opens herself to the possibility of disappointment in love and vows that somehow, some way, she will remain open to it anyway—an extraordinary act of courage. To recognize and take in betrayal—to admit that it is possible no matter how smart or careful you are—and still choose love, is to stand on the razor's edge between wanting safety through love (and holding yourself and your partner hostage to this need) and knowing that such safety is impossible.

Betrayal shakes your sense of trust in the future and undermines your view of the past. It strands you with only one thing to rely on: the present moment. You can't use the present as a tactic to guard against future hurt or to right past wrongs. It simply is what it is. Betrayal shakes your agenda loose from your grip and creates space for magic and a wisdom greater than your own to take over the reins. If all spiritual traditions point to the ability to inhabit the present moment as the only source of joy and wisdom, then betrayal has the unique and fearsome power to usher you through the door.

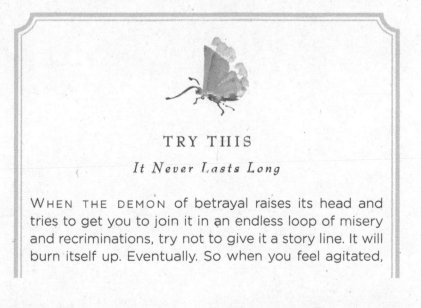

TRY THIS

It Never Lasts Long

WHEN THE DEMON of betrayal raises its head and tries to get you to join it in an endless loop of misery and recriminations, try not to give it a story line. It will burn itself up. Eventually. So when you feel agitated, try to sit with it. Let the agitation be there and make *it* the object of your meditation, just as breath is the object of attention in the Practice of Tranquility. Bring your attention back to the agitation instead of your breath, over and over. Notice where it lives in your body, whether it feels light or dull, cold or hot. Notice how long it lasts. Pay attention and look for the moment it begins to change. This may not sound fun, but try it and see what happens. When I have done it, it tends to shorten the suffering. When the theories and positioning statements arise, don't mock them and don't embrace them. Watch them like your breath. They will come, hang around, and then go. Let them.

13

Of the Four Responses, One Is Helpful

ABOVE ALL, the broken heart searches for reasons. What you had thought gave your life meaning—this person, this relationship and lifestyle—is now gone. Of course you want to know . . . why?! Pain this great must mean *something,* otherwise it's just too cruel. Your mind is so unbelievably agitated that it must occupy itself with something—preferably something that will uncover the secret to getting rid of this pain.

Generally, when trying to make sense of our heartbreak, we take four directions. Only one is helpful.

Blame

First we examine ourselves for fault. If only I had/hadn't done, said, or been this or that, we would still be together. After a while blaming yourself becomes way too anxiety provoking and you turn blame onto the ex. This is actually a good sign. You're beginning to separate yourself from that person. Blaming is an immature effort to kick him out of your life. And he probably is blameworthy in some real ways that are worth examining. Very quickly, however, blaming becomes snide and aggressive and ceases altogether to be illuminating.

Magical Thinking

After blaming comes a kind of analysis that is fruitful, but only up to a point: "What did I ever do wrong that attracted this pain to me? What in my background is so unresolved that I've drawn this heinous situation to myself as a way of finally working it out?" You start to believe that you have the power to attract a healthier relationship to yourself if you can change your mental patterns. On a very profound level, this is true. One does see the world through various lenses, and if one of those lenses somehow reads "kick me," that's not so good. It's important to figure out what you're doing that results in your getting kicked so that you can stop. But this exercise can easily become overly infused with a kind of hope/desperation/superstition that leads you to believe that the moment you hit the right frame of mind, your loved one will present himself to you—and if not, you've screwed up yet again.

Longing/Rage/Becoming Disheartened

Once you exhaust blame and see that magical thinking is not quite as black and white as you'd hoped, it seems only reasonable to go semipermanently on the defensive. Depending on your personality type, this will look primarily like longing, rage, or becoming disheartened. The heartbroken will experience all three, but one of these will be primary. These three poisons are traditionally named passion (or grasping), aggression, and ignorance (or delusion).

Grasping is when every iota you possess of intelligence, attention, and imagination is focused on one thing, and that one thing is *not there*. You could long for him to come back. You could long to feel beautiful again. You could long to return to the boyfriend before him; *he* would never have done this to you. And in a pinch, you can always simply long for love—that you could recover what you had of it in the past or that it would somehow find you in the future. The kaleidoscopic world of sights, sounds, tastes, and impressions is boiled down to one thing: a sign. Whatever occurs is a message—that it was your fault or his, that this happened for a reason or is meaningless, that he is coming back or he isn't, that you *will* find love again, or you *won't*.

If you find that you are interpreting every single thing you perceive as a personal memorandum from the skies about your situation, odds are you have been poisoned by longing.

Longing comes in three sizes: melancholy, gloomy, and miserable. Melancholic longing has sweetness to it, even sexiness; you could find yourself awash in a reverie of the first time you kissed, or simply think again and again of his wonderful qualities and how your life is poorer without them. You could close your eyes and actually smell his scent, taste his skin, almost, *almost* kiss his lips.

At some point, however, melancholy can turn to gloom. Not only do you miss what you don't have, you become increasingly certain you will never have anything like it again and the future looks darker and darker. Everything you do during the course of a normal day—say, shower, eat, work, listen to music—is no longer a simple event but instead is something you will always have to do unaccompanied. You wash your hair and think, *Who cares if it's clean or dirty? There's no one around to bury his nose in it.* As you lift your fork, you see yourself in old age, the only one seated alone in a restaurant on Christmas Day. And so on. Gloom drips from your being like rain from the roof.

Without intercession, gloom easily turns to misery, which is gloom in its solid form. You are certain there is no hope, none whatsoever. Still, underneath this mock certainty is a teeny, tiny glimmer of hope that serves only to immediately make you feel more pathetic. These are examples of the poison of grasping.

What do the three sizes have in common? Complete disavowal of the present moment. When you are longing, you are not here. And longing seems to lead only to more longing, which takes you further and further away. If you could only remember, you would know that in the present moment there is no longing. I'm not just saying that as some kind of hokey-holy new-age (rhymes with sewage) aphorism. It's true. Try it. The antidote to longing is always, always to try to appreciate something that is actually present. If you have a cat, pet the cat. Go out and buy flowers and really take your time choosing them, smelling and touching the petals of all the different varieties. If you use ice cream to drown your sorrow, go get yourself a scoop or three, but this time really taste it. Call a friend and instead of talking about your situation, ask her how she is and really, really try to listen. Even if you can only do it for eight seconds, it will be eight seconds of fresh air. And when you're ready to try again, please do. The eight-second increments will build until you are swayed by a great breeze of cool air.

Those who choose rage as their poison do not feel sad or pathetic at all. They think others are sad and pathetic, not them. They are furious about having their heart broken and are determined it will never, ever happen again. The poison of aggression focuses on one thing and one thing only: *make it go away*.

The handiest way to attempt this is to focus the full intensity of feeling on someone else, the ex, of course, but if he has a new girlfriend, it is an easier, cheaper shot to blame her. (This way you can keep any tender feelings for your ex intact, just in case he decides to come crawling back.) Much time is spent in assignment of blame, no matter who the object is.

Rage is very difficult to counter because, in some ways, it feels good. When caught up in a full-on hissy fit, you feel clear. You feel strong. You feel certain. It's easy to think that you're fighting on the side of right and only saying and doing what everyone would say and do if only she had the guts. Rage also comes in three sizes: it fits the "other woman," him, and yourself.

A friend of mine started dating a man whose fifteen-year marriage had broken up. His ex-wife focused a two-year barrage of insults, threats, hate mail, and insane, accusatory phone calls on my friend at her home and office. My friend eventually obtained a restraining order against this grieving, out-of-control woman. The result was that the ex-wife and her estranged husband had to have frequent conversations about her behavior, during which she could still profess her love for him because it wasn't him she was angry at. No. My friend, whom she had never met, and whom she turned into a full-fledged cartoon Jezebel, was the one she could hate freely.

Ladies. If you are partaking in behavior such as this, I have two words for you: stop it. No matter how much "proof" you have that your love was stolen, it makes no difference. He left. Don't be a chicken. Woman-up. If you are angry, the person to go toe-to-toe with is yourself. Fight for your own heart and don't let it be squashed by anyone: not her, not him, not yourself.

When you direct anger at him, you allow yourself to be filled with thoughts such as . . . well, okay, there's really only one thought, but it has myriad forms: *he deceived me.* Whether by reneging on a marriage proposal, cheating on you, or saying he'll still love you in the morning, he somehow misled you. There is no excuse for this, and I'm not trying to make one. Still, the instruction is the same: stop thinking about what he did and start thinking about what you are going to do to get whole and healthy. Every time you catch yourself thinking, *He is such a jerk, and I will make him pay,* stop. Take a big mental magic marker and X that baby out. Instead, turn your mind to your own behavior, needs, and future.

Finally, you might be tempted to direct anger at yourself. This is not a good idea. It is not the same as taking responsibility for your own feelings. Faulting yourself, regretting your actions, wishing you were prettier/younger/older/smarter/richer: these are not useful activities. Besides, how do you know they're even accurate? Everything is relative. For example, in most of my relationships, I was pegged as the one who always wanted to talk and from whom the words "we need to talk" were ominous portents. But in my current relationship, my wish to converse pales next to my husband's insistence that we stay seated at the table until we get to the bottom of everything and anything. He never, ever lets me escape, and I notice in my fidgeting, avoidance tactics, and sudden, urgent need to sort all the songs on my iPod into playlists, the same shifty-eyed, how-do-I-get-out-of-here reaction I saw in past lovers. So no matter how great a case you make against yourself, know that in a split second, what you dislike in yourself could flip and disappear relative to who your lover is now. Really.

Ultimately, of course, no form of anger is better than another, and they all do more harm than good because anger is always an iteration of something else, a generation removed from its source. Until you get to that "something else," your actions will only create more confusion. So look underneath your anger. No matter whom you're angry at—him, her, or yourself—it is very likely that what you will find is both harder to bear and easier to manage, because it is, finally, the truth: you will find sadness. Allowing sadness to break over you is so difficult and requires much more courage than ranting, raving, and issuing indictments. The antidote to rage is actually sadness. It's allowing yourself to grieve what you have lost because the loss is real. When you are sad, you burn clean fuel. Rage is dirty fuel and simply leads to more and more pollution. So, please, have compassion for yourself and allow yourself to mourn.

The third reaction is becoming disheartened, and in many ways this is the most difficult poison of them all. Even though it seems to have the least charge, unlike longing and rage it is insidious, buried, sticky, and hard to get your arms around. If longing and rage are like burning embers, becoming disheartened is like a weird smell that you can't quite pinpoint and that, eventually, you just get used to. Becoming disheartened is like walking around in the same sweats every day because they're "comfortable." In the indirect grip of this response, you could actually feel relief. It's certainly not as discomfiting as the other two; it doesn't keep you up at night or urge you to have cocktails with breakfast. If under the spell of longing or rage you sob and scream, when you're disheartened, you just sigh and return to watching television. Will you ever love again? Does the future look scary? Meh. Who cares.

Becoming disheartened is actually one of three forms of laziness. (The others are procrastination and being too busy.)

You have simply given up, lost faith in yourself and others, and have chosen, knowingly or not, to cease extending yourself to your world. On a very basic level, and this is the level on which we can begin to clean this up, laziness expresses itself as sloppiness, even lack of hygiene.

So one antidote to disheartenment is simply to clean up your house. Wash your clothes. Comb your hair. Clean out your closets. Okay, that last one may be going too far, but you get what I mean. Try to bring a sense of precision—not militaristic, but kindly attentive—to your activities and environment. When you finish a meal, wash the dishes. When waiting for the bus, have the fare ready. If you've been eating cake three meals a day, substitute a power bar for one of them and at least make sure that the cake is made with the best butter, the best chocolate. If you have done your laundry, put it away. Taking care of details is actually a key antidote to disheartenment. Don't try to get to the bottom of all your psychological problems, just make sure your fingernails are clean. I once heard my teacher say that it's hard to be a spiritual warrior if you can't pick up your clothes. When you begin to care for your environment and your body, you introduce an atmosphere of upliftedness that is the best counter there is to the poignant degradation of a lost heart.

So, to recap: to counter longing, pay attention to the present moment; to counter rage, invite sadness; and to reverse disheartenment, introduce an element of precision to your environment.

Battle

This is the helpful one. At some point, part of your heart will begin to fight to regain some territory. The part of your heart that remains whole starts to do battle with the part that thinks it is broken. Your wish to love and be loved will try to reassert itself. At first this comes through as the voice that won't allow you to linger in any one of the first three stages, which is helpful. It keeps showing you evidence that you are not to blame, he is not to blame, and becoming an asshole or hysteric is not really a great solution. It's very important to locate this voice over and over again. The exercises that follow in this section will help you do this.

Finally, when all the explanations and strategies are worn out, we are simply left with the pain and the wish to love again. Now the work can begin.

14

Act Like a Queen

IN 2007 a book I wrote was up for an award. It was so flattering, but since there was virtually no chance of winning, I wasn't going to travel to Manhattan to attend the ceremony, until I told my mother of the nomination. "We're going!" she shouted. And so we did. My husband, Duncan, and I traveled from Boston, and my parents came in from Washington, D.C. *We'll have a fun weekend together,* I thought, *just so long as everyone understands I am not going to win this award. We'll walk around, try some new restaurants, and I'll get to introduce my husband and parents to a bunch of professional colleagues.*

While in town, we also planned to visit a fancy Fifth Avenue jewelry store where I had once purchased a vintage watch for Duncan. The watch was on the fritz and we wanted some advice. When we got there, the owner, Ed, came over to say hello and, before I could introduce her, my mother said, "Susan's up for an award tonight!"

Without skipping a beat, he asked, "So what are you wearing?" I described a champagne-colored raw silk wrap dress by Calypso. And then he asked, "What's your jewelry?" I'm not a big jewelry person so I shrugged and pointed to the earrings I had on, tiny gold hoops with little bitty dangly things hanging off them. Ed gave me a look that said, "I feel so sorry for you," and with a sigh asked what the neckline on the dress was like. I indicated a deep V. "We'll lend you something," he said. "We do it all the time."

I looked around at the gleaming cases of jewelry with exquisite gems and bold, architectural pieces. My mother looked so excited. I began to get a little excited, too. I'd never worn anything really spectacular in the jewelry department. *Well, okay,* I thought, and I thanked him. We walked around the store as he pulled out piece after gorgeous piece to drape around my neck. "Too big." "Not your color." "Almost." Until finally he held out a necklace that was so gorgeous it actually brought a tear to my eye. It was a thick rope of yellow gold, crusted with tiny rose florets, each one with a diamond in the center. "Perfect," we all said in unison. I looked at myself in the mirror and thought, *This is the most beautiful thing I've ever seen. Maybe I* am *a jewelry person after all.* "Thank you so much, Ed!" "Well, you know it costs fifty-four thousand dollars," he said. "And you'll need earrings to match. Let's keep looking." We all looked at each other, and suddenly I wasn't so sure I was a jewelry person after all. How could I possibly wear something that cost more than a down payment on a home? "Come to the counter," he said. "We just need you to sign something that says we're lending these pieces to you. For insurance purposes."

In case it gets stolen, I thought. *Or I lose it. Or it suddenly explodes during the awards and little golden rose florets go tumbling everywhere while my family and I dive among the ankles of the winners to recover them.* We left the store with a receipt and the jewels in a small shopping bag. It was the strangest feeling to be walking down Fifth Avenue with the equivalent of a couple of new cars in a sack.

As I was getting dressed that night, I realized that there were basically two ways a person could go when wearing a $54,000 necklace. I could wear it with a feeling of embarrassment, of unworthiness, apologetically. Who am I to be wearing such a thing? Or, I could do the opposite: don it proudly, throw my head back, and wear it like, Why shouldn't I be wearing such a thing? Who better than me? But neither of those approaches felt good to me. Then I realized there was a third choice. I could simply wear this astonish-ing piece of jewelry as a thing of beauty, nothing more, nothing less. It didn't mean anything about me—it wasn't too good for me nor was it my due. I didn't have to be a schlump or a diva. Instead, I could be a Queen.

A Queen is a queen no matter what she wears. If she is handed rags, she wears them elegantly. If she is dressed in silks, she wears them with ease. If she is given gems, she says thank you. If she has no gems, she does not feel bereft. Her dignity is self-contained, nat-ural, and independent of outer trappings. Whatever life brings her, she remains seated on her throne.

When your heart is broken, acting like a Queen may not be the first thing you think of. Especially when it comes to relationship heartbreak, you're more likely to act like a brute or a slave. These are not good archetypes to employ when your heart is aching. For example, it may seem like a good idea at the time to call his boss and threaten to have him arrested for sexual harassment (brute), and the next day call him directly and beg to be taken back, saying you'll do anything (slave) if he will—but, believe me, these are not good ideas.

Living with a broken heart, you can learn to be a Queen. The conditions are ripe for leaning into your elegance instead of your despair. In a way, it is your heartbreak itself that introduces you to this elegance. You see that beneath your sorrow is aristocratic gen-tleness and sensitivity—because your heart is so full and rich and deep, it responds so intensely to loss. So instead of acting like a bully or a servant, draw yourself up with the dignity of a Queen, who is not susceptible to what others think of her.

When heartbroken, you need to guard against your own views. When your heart is broken, all you can see is a worthless, unattrac-tive, undeserving loser—the opposite of a Queen.

Here is an exercise to put you in touch with your inner Queen:

Set up two chairs facing each other. Get two pens and two pieces of paper. Sit in one chair with a pen and paper, and then place the other pen and paper on the facing chair.

In your chair, let all the sorrow you feel rise to the surface. It's okay if you cry. Check in with any feelings of worthlessness you might have and let them fill you. Without going into too much detail, very simply write down what about yourself makes you feel ashamed. It could be something like "I'm too needy" or "I'm too unattractive to find love again" or "I deserve this heartbreak." Remember to keep it simple; you don't want to turn this into a self-hate fest.

Now imagine that in the chair opposite you sits your strongest, kindest, most resilient and powerful self. She gazes on you with immeasurable understanding and kindness. Get a sense of her presence, her expression, even her clothing. Put the pen and paper you've been using down on your chair and switch seats. Pick up the new pen and paper and hold them in your lap. Close your eyes and feel what it's like to inhabit *this* you, the one who is so strong and kind and fully alive. Imagine looking at your low-self-esteem self in the opposite chair and let your heart fill with gentleness toward her. Begin to write her a letter telling her what you see. Remind her of all her excellent qualities. Perhaps what she sees as neediness, you, as a Queen, know to be tenderness, and what she calls unattractive, you see as personal and unique. Be specific and be honest. Keep it simple.

When you're done, move back to the original chair with this letter in hand and move the previous letter aside. Get some sense for how you feel right now, in this moment. Then read this missive from your highest self. Really try to take in her words, and when you feel you have done so, imagine these two aspects of yourself blending into one. When you feel this connection has been made, sit up straight like a Queen and know that within you lies sorrow and fragility and power and tenderness and that you are big enough to contain it all.

More Queenly Qualities to help you through your heartache:

• *A Queen knows who she is.*

She is not confused by what others may think of her. She knows her own mind, and no matter how much praise or blame she receives, she is unswayed by either. She knows how to return to center.

• *A Queen does not explain, nor does she complain.*

She has few true confidants. She doesn't make excuses or commiserate. While it can be very, very helpful to tell your story to the right person, spilling it indiscriminately arouses an atmosphere of chaos and victimization. Like a Queen, choose whom you speak to very, very carefully. Take into your confidence only those who can advise you wisely. When you're out and about and are tempted to explain or complain to friends or strangers, think of Queen Elizabeth, preferably as played by Helen Mirren. Can you imagine her whining? Connect with your inner Helen Mirren.

• *A Queen does not attack, she magnetizes.*

In our culture, both men and women are told that the way to get something you want is to go after it and not let anything stop you. This may suit a King, but it's a bit different for a Queen. She knows that the best strategy is not to chase what she wants, but to compel it to come to her through her sense of richness and dignity. Through teaching you to stay within yourself, tracking your thoughts and feelings moment to moment, meditation helps you keep your seat, no matter how stormy the surroundings, and what you seek knows where to find you.

• *A Queen's surroundings are impeccable.*

Okay, so she has handmaidens to hang up her clothes and do the vacuuming. Still, when it comes to a genuine Queen, it's hard to imagine that, left to her own devices, she'd immediately start wearing track suits and allowing dirty dishes to pile up in the sink—things that are very easy to do when you're in a funk. However, no matter how slovenly and icky you feel on the inside, it's important to prevent this from seeping into your environment. The way things look is really important, not from a snobby point of view, but because environment seriously influences mood and expectation. The best environment isn't necessarily one where everything is superfancy and trendy, but one in which it is clear that the inhabitant cares about freshness, beauty, and utility. So definitely keep your place neat and tidy, and no matter how bereft you are, for god's sake, wear clean clothes. Raise the shades, open the windows, bring in fresh flowers, play music—do things to enhance your environment and arrange the palace of the Queen. This will uplift your surroundings and spirit.

• *A Queen is never summoned.*

Not even by her ex. A friend of mine has recently entered into that hell realm known as the on-again, off-again relationship. This is not an unfamiliar story—it's not pretty, but it happens.

When Jessica met Paul, she thought she had hit the jackpot. He was handsome, funny, smart, and on his way to being rich. For a few months, they went out almost every weekend to nice restaurants, the latest movies, parties, and so on. He was great to hang out with and, it turned out, the sexual chemistry was off the charts. At one point, though, she began to wonder if this would ever turn into more than one date a week, followed by sex, which was the pattern they were settling into. After one particularly fun night, she took a chance and asked him where he thought this was going. He sort of shrugged the question off, and Jess got a bad feeling in her stomach. She really, really liked him and wondered if she had messed everything up. Well, perhaps. Paul's reaction was to cut the relationship back from date + sex to just sex. It took a few weeks before she even realized she'd been downsized.

When we talked, she was scared that if she stopped sleeping with him, the relationship would be over. Maybe if she just hung in there a bit longer to give him a chance to get over whatever fright he'd gotten from her "where is this going" question, they could go back to dating and sort of start over again. (Dear readers, what do you think the chances are of that?) First of all, men who scare that easily are simply not worth it. Second of all, a Queen is never summoned. You can't just ring her up and get her to pop over, no matter how delectable the treats are that you are offering. She doesn't say, "How high?" when you say, "Jump!" She has her own life, her own agenda, her own ways of doing things. To give up this privilege is a grievous mistake. No matter how difficult, it is far better to give up a relationship in which you can be summoned than stick around and hope for the best.

15

Give Your Demons a Dinner Party

TIRED OF BATTLING the voices in your head that are alternately telling you you're a loser, he's an asshole, he's the only one for you, you'll never find love, you blew it, it's all _____'s fault? I don't blame you. It is truly exhausting and impossible to try to fight each voice as it arises. It's like trying to fight a flood: you keep bailing, but the waves keep coming. Instead of running around trying to batten every hatch, open them wide and invite the water in.

Make a list of the thoughts that plague you most at this time. Don't try to reason with them or counter them with your excellent logic. Depending on how vicious your inner demons are, you'll probably have three to ten most popular evil thoughts. Write them down. Begin each statement with "I." For example, your thoughts could be things like:

1. I am sad because I'm too old (or ugly or needy or broken) to find a new love.
2. I am furious that he broke his promises and betrayed me.
3. I am petrified that I'll never, ever recover.
4. I always attract commitmentphobes.
5. I am drowning in grief that I have lost this love and nothing will ever replace it.

These are your demons. Instead of trying to shoo them off with a broom, draw yourself up and have a look at them. The surest way to work with the energy of demons is not to combat or ignore them (which simply strengthens them), but to make friends with them. Give each one a name: Shame, Anger, Terror, Disappointment, Grief. Don't get too fancy, just something simple to enable you to differentiate their voices, because they *are* all different. Your heartbreak is not an undifferentiated mess of goo, it is comprised of real sorrows, real psychological history, proper voices that deserve to be heard—but do not let them run the asylum.

If it helps, you can imagine what each one looks like: a tiny child, an enormous horned beast, a twisted dwarf, or they can simply look like you at different stages of your life, or as you are now, each one with a different funny hat. (Look here, they're your demons and you can make them wear whatever you damn well please.)

The fact is, although it may not feel this way, that you are in charge, even of the most overwhelming tidal wave of torment. Here is why I say this: not because you can control it, not because you can transform it, not because you're smarter or deeper or snootier than your most difficult emotion, but because you can *see* it. It can't see you. If you can observe it, you can contain it. If you can observe an emotion or state of mind, you have the possibility of dialoguing with it. If you can dialogue, you can come to an agreement. The one who sees all the emotional chaos is not absorbed in that chaos, and in this exercise we establish our core identity as the one who is surveying the territory, not as those who inhabit it.

Now imagine that you, this *you* who can see all the other feelings, have set a beautiful table with just enough seats for each demon, plus yourself. And set an extra place to your right, for someone whom we will call your spiritual friend. This could be your best friend who always listens to you whether you're happy or sad, or a spiritual figure from whom you've learned things of value, whether in person or through books, movies, or song. So if you have five demons, set seven places. Look each demon in the eye and invite it to dinner. They are all welcome. ("Shame, please come to dinner at my house tomorrow night at 7:00 p.m.") You can close your eyes and picture all this in your head, draw it on a piece of paper, or write it as a little story. ("I am throwing a dinner party and have set the table for seven, myself plus Shame, Grief, etc.")

At the appointed time ask them to sit in the living room as you make sure the table is ready, then invite them to take their seats. Notice what they look like when they enter the room. Are they shaking, giggling, breathing fire? As a good host, you don't comment. You just smile in welcome, show them to their seats, and make sure they're comfortable. This may not be the most fun dinner party you've ever thrown, but you're the host and fun is not your aim, the positive experience of the guests is. So take it easy and know you can eat some chips in front of the tube later, after they're all gone.

After they're all seated, go back to the living room one more time. Is your spiritual friend there? Have a look around the room. What does he or she look like? Please welcome him or her with gratitude.

Now take your seat at the table, with your spiritual friend to your right, or just leave that seat empty. Again, be a good host. Ask each guest to introduce himself and say what he does for work. The truth is each has an important job, one that is meant to be of service to *you*. Demons are simply angels who have been overlooked. When you bring attention to them, they often stop screaming, sobbing, breathing fire, or whatever it is they do, just as a screaming baby who has been left might when you pick it up. For example, Shame may begin by telling you that her job is to remind you that you lack ambition or that your curly hair is the cause of all your problems, but if you press her she may tell you that her job is to keep you in an emotionally contracted state in order to prevent you from exposing yourself to hurt. Anger may say his aim is to scare away anyone who might threaten you. Allow each to speak. Listen carefully. When each demon is done, ask him if there is anything else he wants to tell you or ask of you. What does this demon require in order for you to see it? What can you honor this demon for? If the demon just can't be calmed down, don't go over to offer comfort or run away in fear. Simply hold your seat at the head of the table, move on to the next guest, and come back to the vociferous one later. If dialogue is still not possible, simply gaze kindly at this one.

At the end, turn to your spiritual friend to see if she has anything to add. If so, listen. If not, just be grateful for her silent support. Finally, thank everyone for coming and show them to the door. Hug your spiritual friend as the last to leave. The party is over.

The act of making friends with demons is a radical act. It is radical because you are choosing to look at what is terrorizing you rather than plotting to triumph over it; you're going against most of the recommendations from the world of self-help. All strategies are, at first, nothing more than an effort to run from yourself. And you're already feeling abandoned enough; don't you abandon you, too.

There is only one strategy for working with negative energy, and that is to open yourself to it. You will learn many things, but this knowledge is not what shifts the balance of power between you and your demons—what does is the simple act of opening itself. There is enormous value in doing so. In fact, openness is the greatest source of personal power that you will ever find. And every brokenhearted gal needs to feel her power restored.

16

Expect Jeannie

I WAS TALKING to a friend the other day about the guy she
had been dating for the last six months. She really, *really* liked him,
and everything had been going along swimmingly (including awe-
inspiring sex, shared likes and dislikes, and allusions to future
shared events) until, mysteriously, he stopped returning her calls.
Like, completely. (Why the *hell* do people do things like that??) For
whatever reason, this relationship was over—just like in fashion:
one day you're in and the next you're out. Auf Wiedersehen.

We both knew what she was in for now. We settled in for the
siege of the broken heart. Sleepless nights. Obsessive email checking. Radical weight loss. Bouts of sobbing brought on by bad pop
songs. And as her best pal, I knew what I was in for: Many crying
phone calls. Listening to her try to puzzle her way through what
happened—a thousand times. Trips to her place with takeout at the
drop of a hat. Making sure I had plenty of good DVDs for her
when she wanted to come cry on my couch and then hang out. I
had no issues with doing this for her because I loved her, but also
because someone had done this for me when I needed it most—and
I will never forget that kindness and how much it helped.

When I was going through heartbreak hell, a woman named
Jeannie came to my rescue. We had worked together for several

years but were not all that close. One day, when we happened to be the only two in the office, I broke down and confided in her. She was so kind and such a wonderful listener. From then on she paid special attention to how I was feeling. She noticed me when I came to work and greeted me with a wink and a smile, to let me know she was thinking of me. I discovered that I could call her at any hour and she would be so generous and listen to me, even though I basically told the same story over and over. (Why did he do this? Do you think it was because I said or did _____? Do you think he misses me?) Each time, she listened as if it were the first time, and each time I felt my pain lessen.

It's not unusual for one particular friend to surface during the time of heartbreak as your number one confidante. It may or may not be someone you expect. It could be someone already very close to you or, as I often have noticed, someone with whom you weren't all that close until now. Sometimes a friend just comes to you out of the blue.

Before this awful breakup, I knew people were nice, but I didn't know how nice they really were, even my own friends. I was amazed at how kind some people were. (And how uncaring others were—emotional crises provide immediate B.S. detection among your peers. It may be surprising who comes to your side and who waits it out.)

And it wasn't only Jeannie who showed up for me. I had one friend who, when I called her to tell her I was about to lose it at work, would dash over, pull up outside my office, and leave the car in neutral. I'd run down, jump in, and cry my eyes out while she handed me tissues. Then I'd jump out, go back to my desk, and she'd go back to work without a word. Another friend, who owned a bar, would drive by my house after closing time—if he saw my lights on, he'd know I was having another sleepless night and come in, give me a hug, and tell me how stupid my ex-boyfriend was for giving me up. Connecting over and over with someone who cares enough to listen—not to agree or to counsel or to explain, but just to listen—is amazingly therapeutic. Nothing changes, on one hand, but somehow telling the story is like exposing a film negative to the light—each time you do, it becomes fainter and fainter.

After I realized how great it was to tell the story (which is different somehow from complaining and whining), I wanted to tell it as much as possible. Understandably, I became afraid of wearing out my current friends, even the amazing Jeannie. So I hired some new ones. I saw therapists, astrologers, body workers, trainers; I basically had a team working on my case around the clock. I told the story of my heartbreak to each of them. And you know what? Each time I did, the pain eased up a little more.

If you can afford it, I highly recommend this. You can also log on to websites and rail about your pain on forums for the brokenhearted. You can start your own blog, just to rant. Use a fake name if you're too embarrassed to claim your railings. Go on Twitter, name yourself "Sob Sister," and tweet your sorrow 24/7, 140 characters at a time. People will respond with kindness. This is a very important thing to remember as you navigate your own broken heart or help a friend with hers. *Kindness really helps.* Remember, Jeannies are everywhere.

17

Become Wrathful

ANGER IS THE WORST of the afflictive emotions because, more than the others, it can lead to violence. Anger causes people to lose control, terrify those around them, destroy furniture, and, in the very worst case imaginable, do physical or emotional harm to another person. When you get angry, you lose a sense of other people's humanity and see them instead as evil pawns in your internal theater. They appear as mere devices to either inflame or dispatch your own feelings of rage. And when you forget that other people are human beings, *even* the bastard that broke your heart, very bad things happen.

A few years ago I was driving to the market in my town. To enter the market, you have to go through a traffic rotary, which in Boston is like an invitation to play bumper cars. I have an insanely stupid pet peeve about rotaries: when people do not respect the laws about entering them (those in the rotary have the right of way!!!!), I become incensed. No, that's too polite. I become enraged. Of all the nutty things Boston drivers are capable of, this is the one that sends me over the edge. (I'm not proud of this, believe me.)

So one sunny Sunday morning I was on my way to the market when a beat-up black Dodge Charger circa 1990 came barreling into the rotary *when I was already in there, lawfully holding the right of way.* Imagine. The car cut me off, and I leaned on my horn, gave the finger, shouted epithets, and generally acted like a lunatic. If I could have pushed a Medusa button, I gladly would have caused snakes to emanate from my head, spitting and threatening this, this *Dodge Charger.*

I was gratified when I saw it was also heading to the market so I could keep haranguing it and, not removing my hand from the horn, pulled up right beside it in the parking lot, ready to scream. (Please forget you ever heard this story.) I went to roll down my window, and as I did, looked at the driver. I saw a young woman who appeared to be from another country with a truly terrified look on her face. In the backseat, her baby was belted into a car seat. He was sobbing uncontrollably. I froze. I recognized that I had made this baby cry and frightened this poor, poor lady. By this time my window was rolled down and the angry words were caught in my throat. Still, I opened my mouth, but what came out was, "I'm sorry. I'm sorry. Please forgive me." Her face relaxed a tiny bit, but instead of entering into a dialogue with me about how screwed up I was, she quite understandably closed her window and got the hell out of there. I rolled up my window, too, and cried my eyes out. How could I have been such a jerk? I hurt her and I hurt her little baby. I felt bad for several days, actually even up until right now, come to think of it.

So this is a tiny example of how anger works. I didn't see a woman and a baby when my anger rose, I saw a Dodge Charger. Without noting that humans were involved, I felt free to inflict pain. The moment I saw their faces, the whole thing dissipated and all I felt was tenderness toward them and outraged disappointment in myself. (Imagine what happens when collective anger is directed, not toward a single person, but toward a religion, nation, or ethnic group. We don't even have to imagine. We can see proof all around us.)

There is one very particular (and tricky) sense, however, in which anger can be helpful. I think of it as an advanced skill and therefore apply it very, very infrequently, but when your heart is broken and you've fallen into a depression, sometimes you need to throw a little hand grenade in there to get yourself out. Employing this tactic successfully hinges on maintaining an impeccable sense of the humanity of all beings, including (especially) yourself. When anger is in service of compassion, i.e., it is an extension of caring rather than absorption in one's personal agenda, it can be powerfully beneficial. Think: mother yelling at child about to touch hot stove. That kind of thing. This is called the power of wrath.

In Buddhist iconography, very beautiful, dignified people sit in the posture of meditation, looking extremely composed. They are peaceful manifestations of compassion. But there are other kinds of images, too, scary, threatening beings, perhaps with one eye, fangs, or several heads, holding skulls or standing on top of people. According to Buddhist legend, these images depict creatures who made an oath to protect the teachings of the Buddha. They are the wrathful expression of compassion. Their enemy is ignorance and its brothers: anger, fear, and hysteria. When you exhibit these behaviors, their anger is against you. When you act with compassion and others threaten you with these things, their anger is against them. This is why they are called protectors.

When your heart is broken, the energy of wrathfulness has its place—not through expressing anger against whomever may have hurt you, but as a way of cutting through laziness, whininess, pettiness, or excessive self-absorption that may be trapping you in a state of emotional deadness. Emotional volatility is what you're after here. While it's important to allow your feelings to be as they are, it's also possible to confuse honest self-reflection with reflexive self-pity. A good litmus test to tell the difference is your sense of humor. I've noticed that, no matter how sad I am, when my feelings of grief are genuine and in the moment, I can still find a way to laugh at myself if someone is good enough to say something silly about my situation. When I'm simply indulging my negativity and feeling supersorry for myself, any attempts to make light are taken as grievous insult.

When wrath is used to cut through self-pity, defuse self-doubt, and dispel self-absorption, it is a kind friend indeed. You could use it to get yourself off the couch and to the gym. It could help you decide against *another* night of Lifetime Television movies for women and instead go out with friends. And it could compel you to give up tending to your sorrow and instead, for a while, tend to the sorrow of others by volunteering with a charitable organization or simply reaching out to a friend who may also be struggling with some difficulty. You will be amazed by the extent to which wrath will help you to help others and, therefore, yourself. The precious quality of wrath can help you leap the chasm that you may imagine separates you from the rest of humanity.

18

Intensify to Let Go

ONE SUNDAY NIGHT I got a text from my friend Julie, sent via BlackBerry. She was on the subway in NYC, crying. She and her boyfriend had broken up over six months ago, and she thought she was doing great when one of those unseen tidal waves of grief washed over her, perhaps provoked by some evil subway ad or the way the person sitting across from her was chewing her gum. (Anything can spark one of these waves...) "He was the first one who ever made me feel beautiful, and I just don't think I'll ever feel that way again," she said. She felt that her beauty was somehow bestowed by his embrace and, embrace withdrawn, her beauty dissolved.

I emailed her back: "You're just as attractive and wonderful as you were before and during this relationship. Only now you get to be more beautiful because you have tasted the depths of your own tenderness and fragility. This is the kind of thing that gives outer beauty soul and creates inner beauty that cannot be compromised."

This is obviously not true just for the beautiful Julie. It is true for you, too. No matter how swollen your face with tears or fat or skinny you have (momentarily) become, the inner light is lit by owning your inner life completely.

Anyone experiencing heartbreak is familiar with the unpredictable swells of grief and sorrow that can arise from nowhere. They can be invoked by something understandable (watching a sad love story on TV) or something that makes no sense (choosing a cell-phone plan—they asked if you wanted the Friends & Family plan and it made you sad). Sometimes the rush of feeling happens when you're at home alone or driving in your car, which is quite convenient, because you have some privacy. But other times are extremely *in*convenient, like sitting around a conference table with your colleagues or standing in line at the grocery store. What can you do when you simply can't afford to break down? This very brief exercise can be done on the spot, anywhere, and is meant to work with the emotions directly as a way of setting them aside for now. It may sound counterintuitive at first, but try it a few times to see for yourself if it's useful.

TRY THIS
Intensify, Intensify, Let GO

AS SOON AS YOU FEEL that the awful feeling (sorrow, rage, anxiety) is about to make an entrance, immediately tune into it as fully as you can. Invite it in. Feel it. Locate any bodily sensation that may be associated with it. Does it seem to be located in your stomach? Chest? Head? Take its pulse: if this feeling had a heart, would it be racing, pounding, or about to expire? Whatever it is, turn your attention to it as fully as you're able—and intensify it. Purposely amp it up. Imagine that you're lighting a match to it. If the feeling is hot, make it burn. If it's cold, let it turn to ice. If it's speedy, rev the engine. Intensify. Intensify. And then—poof!—let it go. Just like when you open a super-clenched fist, you should feel a sense of cool relief, no matter how momentary. Remember: Intensify. Intensify. And then let it go. Repeat as often as you need to.

19

Trump This

THIS IS ONE OF THE very best ways I know of to deal with emotional pain, no matter how severe. It sounds very simple and it is—although it isn't easy. In fact, the ability to consistently replace painful thoughts with nonpainful thoughts is a sign of excellent psychological attainment. With practice, you can certainly do this for yourself.

The objective is to catch painful thoughts, and instead of allowing them to have their way with you, dig them up on the spot and plant a different thought. There is a way to do this that brings healing and, however, a way to do it that creates more suffering.

Our culture places a lot of emphasis on positive thinking—on assuming that things will work out in your favor, that no challenges will arise, and if they do, these challenges should be recast as further evidence of your power, not your failing. I once had a boss who refused to entertain talk of problems or failure. Problems could be spoken of only as opportunities, and failures as challenges. He actually forbade the use of the word *but* in conversation. If you wanted to point out a problem with a particular strategy (such as, "But that will never work because it will cost ten thousand dollars and our budget has allocated five hundred dollars), you had to use the word *and*. ("And that will never work because . . .") *And* was not much better than *but* because every time someone said, "and," we knew he or she meant "but." And I digress.

I'm not a huge fan of this. False optimism seems rather immature and superstitious. So-called negative thoughts are not banished simply by replacing them with wishful thoughts. We can have the confidence to entertain the possibility of having a problem without falling apart or feeling cursed. Instead of replacing "I'll never love again" with "I will, too, love again," I think it's better to go with something like "I may love again; I just don't know at this point." Or, "Right now, what I love is _____." You can fill in the blank with anything you want, as long as you genuinely love it. It could be "that my friends care about me," "this cupcake," or "the pink flower outside my window." Trying to fight with the idea of "I'll never love again" by countering with "I will, *too,* love again" simply prolongs the pain. Instead of fighting with your thought, trump it with a better one. A better thought is one that you *know* is true, pertains to this very moment, or that turns you into a more loving person. Here are a few more examples:

I don't think I can make it through this day could become *I know I can make it to the next breath.*

I have serious flaws that will prevent me from ever finding love could become *What I love about me is that I'm always trying to become a better person.*

He's an evil, bad, dreadful, criminally horrible person could become *I hope that everyone on earth who is currently feeling victimized and betrayed could find peace. Including me.*

Trump that.

20

Mirrors

THE POINT OF THIS EXERCISE is to connect you more firmly with both your strength *and* your heartache. When your heart is broken, you think that all of you is broken and that you're always going to be broken. It isn't permanent. It's very helpful to know that there is something within you that is larger than both the pain and the strength. This larger self can hold it all, just as the sky can hold rain clouds and sun, deep darkness and the light of the moon.

Find a place to sit quietly where you won't be disturbed. Make yourself comfortable and close your eyes. If you start to cry at any time during this exercise, no problem. Just allow it.

Picture yourself in a room with three mirrors. You can imagine them any way you like. See yourself standing in front of all three. Look in the first mirror and connect with yourself as you are when your heart is not broken. Look at the woman in the mirror closely. What does she look like? Does she appear strong, carefree, relaxed, intent, or something else? Take her in. Allow an ocean of strong, wholehearted people to gather around her, all those who have had their hearts broken and gotten over it. These could be people you know, people you've read about, or just the sense that in the world there are countless people who have mended their own hearts. Let your energy blend with theirs. Let the person in the mirror take her place in the lineage of spiritual warriors who have strong hearts.

Now turn your gaze to the second mirror and see your face as the one who is suffering a broken heart. Really take yourself in; if there is a sense of despair, hopelessness, anger, whatever it may be, look into the face of the one whose heart is broken. Really feel into this quality of shattered heart. If it helps, you can place your hand on your chest over where you feel your heart to be. Tune into any physical sensations of heartache. Allow the legion of people who are also suffering from broken hearts to gather around you, whether known to you or unknown.

Don't connect to their pain. Connect to their (and your own) wish to be loved. Acknowledge this wish as honorable and good. Know that you are part of a lineage of deeply loving people. If you weren't able to love deeply, your heart would not ache so much. So check in with your tenderness and fragility. Notice if your image in the mirror has changed. Let her take her place in the lineage of spiritual warriors who have borne their own sorrow, who have allowed themselves to be this deeply touched by another person.

Finally, turn to the third mirror. Let each of your previous images—the strong-hearted you and the brokenhearted you—step out of their frames and into this third mirror. Let these energies—abiding emotional fortitude and sweet tenderness—mix. Attune to this coexistence and feel its texture. Take it into yourself, the one who is gazing into the mirror. Breathe it in and relax with it.

Now let all the mirrors go blank. Turn around and walk away. Sit quietly for another minute or two, or as long as you like.

21

"I Forgive You"

MY FRIEND LILLY, like me, like you, like everyone, sometimes has problems with low self-esteem. Without notice or reason, a magazine ad for shampoo or a colleague's two-second delay in responding to her morning greeting can cause her to suddenly become awash in shame, self-judgment, feelings of inadequacy—the usual. When your heart is broken, it is especially easy to be toppled by the slightest input into a swamp of self-recrimination. Besides being untrue, vile, and unhelpful, this internal commentary makes you believe that you have committed some sin that, until repented, brands you as unworthy of love. Too ugly. Too pretty. Too uncaring. Too caring. Shouldn't be so nervous. Should be more Zenlike. And so on.

In her effort to combat such feelings, Lilly discovered an incredibly simple, totally useful, on-the-spot way to neutralize feelings of worthlessness. The moment a thought arises, such as "I wish I hadn't said that," or "If only I wasn't so (needy, chubby, tall, ambitious)," she simply says to herself, "I forgive you." Each and every time she catches one part of herself trying to talk the rest of her into believing that she's made some grievous mistake or is indeed comprised solely of grievous mistakes, she lets herself off the hook with these three simple words. "I shouldn't have tried to get him to meet my family so early in our relationship." I forgive you. "If I had known the pressure he was under, I would have been more supportive when he talked about his problems at work." I forgive you. "I could have been more patient about his reluctance to commit." I forgive you. The "I forgive you" method is particularly useful in response to any internal line of reasoning that begins with "shoulda, woulda, or coulda."

I've tried this method and it works. I have yet to encounter anything I cannot forgive myself for, just as I would forgive a dear friend who might exhibit the same quality. The next time a feeling of remorse or regret comes up, try forgiving yourself. You're only human, after all.

22

Really Unhelpful Things

NOW ON TO THE THINGS that do *not* help.

Relationship Replay

This is what my friend Sarah calls it when you're sitting at your desk or lying in bed minding your own business, and suddenly you begin ruminating (for the umpteenth millionth time) over what you did right and he did wrong that led to the breakup, or vice versa, what you did wrong and he did right. If only you hadn't rolled your eyes when he said he would pick you up after work. If only you hadn't pushed him to make it to that dinner with your mother or buy those pants. Everything would have been fine, if only.

No, it wouldn't have. The temptation to ruminate endlessly on specific moments, conversations, and outfits is nearly irresistible. I don't know why these replays are so compelling because they are just so completely unhelpful. They're especially unhelpful when you are by yourself; somehow spilling your ruminations to a pal is (somewhat) better because once you've gotten it out on the table, it seems easier to move on. If you're lucky, you have a friend who doesn't mind hearing the story over and over. When it's just you, the thoughts can go in endless, pitiless, punishing circles.

"Helpful" Friends

Almost everyone has had her heart broken and has had to figure out how to deal with it. Some people do better than others. It's not uncommon to respond to heartbreak with bitterness, cynicism, self-pity, and investment in many self-help books. Sometimes people arrive at pretty firm conclusions about what heartbreak means and what you should do about it.

While it can be extremely empowering to talk to the right person, it is *not* helpful to talk to people who corroborate your negative thoughts or aspire to put such thoughts in your head where they weren't before. It is also not helpful to talk to people who want to explain to you why you feel so terrible and then tell you that the *only* way to get over it is to go skydiving, schedule a colonic, or stop eating dairy. These are the wrong people.

Expressing Yourself Isn't Always a Great Idea

After our breakup, I wrote my ex-boyfriend a ten-page, single-spaced, tear-stained, exclamatory letter detailing his every insufficiency and, when I couldn't get him to come to the phone so I could read it to him (imagine that), I drove over to his house, banged on his door, and demanded that he Come. Outside. Right. Now. Which he did, with an air of stunned resignation. He shut the door behind him, took me by the arm, and walked me to the curb where I read the entire letter to him, interrupted by sobs of despair, partly over our breakup and partly over how deeply untouched he was by my tirade. He waited for me to finish and then went back inside. Nothing had changed.

As I drove home, I felt a curious combination of relief and increased grief. When you're suffering under the burden of heartbreak, intense, indescribable anxiety arises and you would do anything to alleviate it, anything. For some strange and sad reason, confronting your ex—or having any contact with him at all—can provide momentary relief. After all, when you've spent hours and hours and days and nights thinking of someone, seeing him is actually a break from the tedium of endless rumination about him. It's like you've spent a thousand hours in the ring shadowboxing and long to connect with an actual opponent. It just feels so good to hit something besides air. It's tempting to want to connect with the one who hurt you, as I exhibited in my shameful example.

But ultimately, taking this action created way more sorrow for me because I saw that no matter how hard I swung, no punch would ever connect with him. He was simply outside of my reach; nothing I did affected him. This is how it is when, for one person, a relationship is over. All he can do is look at the person for whom it is not over and shake his head. You are simply in two different worlds now. It is over.

The temptation to lure him back into a shared world through seduction, manipulation, and begging is strong. You have been trapped by his choice about your relationship and, instead of asserting dominion over your world by making your own choices, you allow his choice to enslave you.

Nothing Matters, Everything Sucks, Please Don't Try to Talk Me Out of This

It can happen that you are so deeply, deeply hurt that believing there is no hope is actually the safest place you can find to hide. It's just too risky to invest even one molecule of openness in the possibility of happiness because it could be dashed in a nanosecond.

I totally understand this. When I've been at my lowest, the lowest of all time, I've sought those who are likely to give me reassurance just so that I could shoot them down. It gave me a perverse sort of pleasure to do this. They would say, "Don't worry, there is someone out there for you." "No, there isn't," I'd say (or think). "And if there were, he'd turn out to be a he-man woman hater like all the rest. No thank you." "This experience will make you stronger." "I don't want to be stronger; I just want to be happy and besides, it's not making me stronger, it's destroying me." "He wasn't good enough for you anyway." "Yes, he was, yes, he was, yes, he was. You just couldn't see his fantastic qualities like I could." "You're still lovely and sexy." "Ha! Ha! Ha! If I were, he'd still be here. I'm an ugly, dried-up hag. Can't you see that?"

Each opportunity to whack their kind sentiments right back in their faces further entrenched me in my cave of thick, black tragedy. Don't get me wrong; losing love is so dark and sad, it is absolutely worthy of intense grief. But there is a difference between mourning that is genuine and honest, and willfully holding on to anguish, which is cowardly. I've spent many days and even months (years?) gripping my hopelessness, not because I thought it was warranted, but because letting go even for one second and allowing myself to once again be touched by the desire for love was simply too risky. It seems easier to stay cooped up in your stinky old house than to open the door and walk out into the fresh air.

As mentioned earlier, this is a form of laziness. Laziness has several definitions, one of which is called "becoming disheartened." Yes, losing heart, losing faith in yourself and in life, is a sign of laziness because you have chosen to hide rather than step out into the light and perhaps risk everything.

My friend Lindsay has had her heart broken more times than anyone should ever have to suffer. Really. She is a beautiful, talented, successful, sexy woman who seems to get involved with people who don't value her. While there may be some deep-seated psychological wound begging to be healed, there is also the simple fact that these things have happened and, ultimately, no one really knows why. But this doesn't stop her from searching for answers, and for this I value her enormously. She reads books, gets therapy, takes healing vacations, and will basically visit any shaman, counselor, or therapist who can treat her deepest woundings. I totally commend this and have seen her gain remarkable insight from her explorations. However, through all her searching, she has concluded that there is almost no hope—not until she gets her act totally together, and until such time, she's going to stay safely indoors, out of relationships, thank you very much. She thinks she's being smart, but instead of taking refuge in love and faith, she has taken refuge in despair. She has fallen victim to becoming disheartened-as-laziness, to using her quest for love as a shield against love.

Although it is terrifying, it is also liberating to learn that there is no such shield.

OTHER DEEPLY UNHELPFUL THINGS

- Overanalyzing his behavior and motivations
- Playing the blame game
- Thinking you should be okay when you're not
- Screwing around with the wrong people (though screwing around with the right people *can* help. Not to be cavalier or anything)
- Emoting all the time
- Revenge
- Denial
- Saying bad things about him
- Saying bad things about yourself
- Driving past his house to see if his lights are on
- Avoiding/seeking places where he might show up
- Calling someone's boss and trying to get her fired (I know someone who did this—to me.)
- Showing up at parties you weren't invited to and looking really scary and mean (I know someone who did this—me.)

It is very helpful to have a strategy already lined up for when such urges arise. The most important thing is to introduce an interruption between your thought (*I'm going to drive over there right now. Naked.*) and action (searching for your keys while pulling off your clothes). There are three choices:

- Ask one of your friends to be the designated, go-to person who has promised to talk you down from any crazy plans. Call him.
- Do the crazy, unhelpful thing you're thinking about, but only

on paper. Imagine yourself doing whatever you're considering and write it out, in detail. You can approach this as a realist: "What would happen if I actually did this action?" Or you can approach it as a fantasy: "What do I wish would happen?" Get as outrageous as you want. Just don't do it in real life.

- Turn your attention directly *toward* the pain that is just beneath the surface of your call to action. If you're about to diss him to some friends, recognize that you're really seeking allies to fortify yourself and your position. If you are getting stuck in ruminations about your past behavior and what you wish you had done differently, tune in to the sense of helplessness that comes with trying to change the past. If you're about to serve him with a two-thousand-word email detailing every one of his failings, step away from the send button and connect instead with the fury you feel about being abandoned, ignored, or simply forgotten.

As soon as you locate the right emotion, drop any narrative you've constructed around it and instead try to time how long the feeling itself lasts. Literally. Look at your phone or computer or anything with a clock on it and see how long you can hold on to this particular emotion. Hold on as long as you can. Hold it. *Hold it.* How long before it simply begins to change on its own? At some point, no matter how hard you concentrate on that difficult emotion, your mind will slip into another line of inquiry such as, "I wonder what's for dinner" or "I've really got to get my laundry done." You won't be able to help it. When this happens, check your timer. See how long your feeling lasts before it simply begins to fade. Rest assured that at some point, no matter how many crazy things you're contemplating, each and every one of the feelings underlying them will all fade away.

23

Really Untrue Things

HERE IS A LIST OF THINGS you may try to get yourself to believe when you are heartbroken that are simply not true. Or remotely useful. How many have flashed through your mind? What would you add to this list? When one of these arises in your mind, no matter how many times it happens, look yourself in the eye and say, "I have no way of knowing if this is really true. And P.S. *Hello:* not helpful."

1. He was the only one for me.
2. I'm too old and this was my last chance.
3. I'm going to end up pathetic and living alone in a trailer.
4. He/she is really gay/straight and doesn't know it.
5. I'll never love again.
6. I am too flawed to deserve love.
7. He was too flawed to love me right.
8. If he doesn't love me anymore, I'm not lovable.
9. If my (mother, father, aunt, teacher, boss, electrician) hadn't been so (demanding, withdrawn, angry, uncaring) this never would have happened to me.

10. If I hadn't said, done, or thought _____, this wouldn't have happened.
11. This was the real thing. And I blew it.
12. My love was too powerful and he couldn't handle it.
13. One day he will get his and I will feel so much better.
14 I have problems with intimacy.
15. He has problems with intimacy.
16. If only I had not been too blinded by love to see that he was a liar/womanizer/dope dealer/Republican/Democrat/mama's boy, I wouldn't have made this mistake.
17. If only I had listened to so-and-so (my mother/preacher/book club/life coach) this never would have happened.
18. My/his unresolved psychological issues made love impossible.
19. I attracted this pain by thinking the wrong thoughts.
20. One day he'll see that my love was the best thing that ever happened to him. In the meantime, f&*k him.

24

Intimacy Is Always There

WHAT YOU FEEL when love is lost, though akin to other losses, is different from what you feel when a loved one dies, or your house burns down, or you find out that you are ill. What, ultimately, could be at the bottom of this unique strain of heartbreak?

Although it is always unique and personal on one hand, on the other, it seems to hit those who suffer it in largely the same way. While we may react differently on the surface—some become enraged and go off like loose cannons, some fall into a stiff, despairing depression, while others go numb and allow themselves to die a little on the inside—underneath these responses is something we have in common that makes it so devastating and, at the same time, a profound path to wisdom. What we have lost reveals our most hidden longing: to be fully and thoroughly met.

To be "met" obviously doesn't mean in the "how are you, nice to meet you" sense. Instead, it means something deeper. It means that the totality of who you are is received into the being of another, causing that other to open his arms to you and extend the perfect shelter of sacred acceptance. It is sacred in that it is unconditional. It ignores faults and assets alike and reaches through them to simply hold *you*. You feel that you can fully come into existence by such an embrace. It is what we all long for, and this longing animates us in motion and in stillness, awake and asleep, in a relationship or not. It is intrinsic and very mysterious.

Almost every night, I have the same dream. In the course of doing something mundane like going to a meeting or sitting on an airplane, I meet a stranger and a feeling of mutual rapture suddenly arises. There is an overwhelming wish to touch and be touched. It is a magnetic pull that suddenly shrinks the entire world into one-pointed focus: the possibility, never quite realized, of bliss. I have had this dream all my adult life, and in recent years it truly is an almost nightly occurrence. I have no idea what it means, really. I wake up next to my husband and sneak into his arms, whether to approximate the bliss-embrace or brush it away as unreal, I don't know. To lie in his arms is my greatest pleasure, but it is not the same. The desire to be in that precise moment of magnetic and pure connection to another, over and over, is, perhaps, hardwired.

When it comes to losing love, it is losing the possibility of this moment that causes such powerful suffering. When you think about what you have lost, it is likely not the funny jokes you shared, but the moment when your minds met to see the humor together. It is probably not the fun evenings out at your favorite club that you miss, but the sense of special, unspoken alignment with this other person, the two of you bound by an unseen link, made even more precious amid the chaos of crowds and loud music. And it probably isn't even the future that you grieve (with the house and the vacations and the cozy gatherings with friends), but the sense of going forward with another into the future, shoulder to shoulder, creating one world together. It is that feeling of being met and accompanied right here, right now, and into the foreseeable future, that we hunger for. We'll compromise a lot to hold on to this promise.

I can prove it to you that it's not your ex that you are missing so much, but the possibility of sacred connection you sensed with him. I can totally prove it. No matter how special, wonderful, one-of-a-kind superior this lost person is, *the moment you feel the possibility of this connection with another, the person you now miss will disappear entirely from your consciousness*. Really. All the superspecific yearnings you now experience—for the smell of his neck, the particular rumble in his voice, his sleepy face in the morning—will simply dissolve. As if they had never been there. You may not believe me right now, but it's true. And at some point in the future, you will look back and go, "I felt those things about *him?*" I'm not saying you won't retain a melancholic and legitimately grievous sense of loss, but it will be nostalgia, not a present longing. Because what you are missing is not him. What you are missing is the superpowerful and utterly genuine thrill of intimacy. And rightly so. It is something to be longed for, cherished, and, certainly, grieved when it is lost.

But here's the thing. The person who you lost does not hold the key to this sense of connection. Even if you were to spend the next forty years with him, you would not find that thing that you actually long for, except in very special moments. I mean, look at the reality of your relationship. When you were together, did you feel this special connection every moment? Of course not. You likely saw his good and bad points, and when the amazing moments of communion came along, they left you enraptured and then you noticed that he needed a haircut or remembered that you had to do some laundry. That's how life is. But somehow when your heart is broken, all you remember are the rapturous moments. I know that sometimes people think it will help you to heal if you retrospectively catalogue those moments as bogus, but I don't think so, because they were real. And now they're gone. The nutty thing is that even if you were still together, this would still be true.

Instead of (or in addition to) crying all the time because of how much you miss the sense of being connected to another, if you look around, you can see that such moments of intimacy are occurring all the time. Okay, okay, so they don't (usually) involve happily taking your clothes off, but still, they're quite lovely, profound, and, if you pay attention, satisfying. They happen when you're standing in line at the market and you catch another customer's eyes to grin at an overheard conversation. When you're reading a book and suddenly one line jumps out as if it were speaking directly and only to you. Or when you're listening to music and a certain tone or chord progression seems to mirror your state of soul exactly. When you meet a friend for lunch and see that she understands exactly what you are feeling and your hearts open together into a state of closeness. Sure, these moments may leave you wishing for more when they are gone, but that's how life goes. They're never permanent. It's actually quite freeing to realize that.

Just now, writing that last sentence, a lovely warm breeze blew across my back as I sit on a settee by an open window in the Colorado Rockies. It's early on a July morning and I'm all alone. I'm wearing a thin nightgown, which leaves most of my back bare, and I have a blanket around my legs to provide just enough warmth against the cool mountain air. The way the breeze touched my back was so private, it was as if the sky itself reached down to touch me, only me. It took me by surprise, just like in my dreams. The world is always trying to touch you in this way.

Intimacy is always there. You just have to look. I'll have to remember to tell this to my dream boyfriend the next time I see him.

Part
Three

Be Where You Are

25

A Luminous Journey

WHILE WRITING THIS BOOK I noticed that every time I mentioned the title, whoever I was speaking to would get a far-away look in her eyes. I could see her travel back to her own experience of brokenheartedness. Whatever we were doing at the time—walking down the street, taking a drive, dining out, sitting on an airplane—the hustle and bustle of everyday life would stop and she would look away. Any trace of hardness or distance would disappear and her whole being would become soft. "Oh," she would say. "Oh. That happened to me once," and we would look at each other in a new way, like siblings instead of strangers.

Everyone who has gone through genuine heartbreak, the kind addressed in this book, the kind you are experiencing, where life as you know it basically ceases to work, has had the experience that you, the reader, are going through. They couldn't eat, sleep, or work without tremendous difficulty. They believed their lives were over and that love would never, ever come to them again, or, if it did, it would be but a faint version of what they had just lost. And you know what? Of the many people I spoke to about their broken hearts, none of them—*none of them*—ended up giving up on love itself. And all of them, when looking back on the experience of having a broken heart, felt that they were in a different world during that time. (And, please note, none of them still has that alienated feeling.) Every one of them has moved beyond her heartbreak. Each one has healed sufficiently to seek new love or even to be found by it. These things will happen to you, too. You will move past this. You will, you will, you will.

I also noticed that when people were suddenly reminded of their own heartbreak and flashed back to the reality of that time, instead of looking back with bitterness, a kind of sweetness and melancholy seemed to overtake them. Although it sounds clichéd, they were grateful for the experience. I could see that, instead of considering their broken heart as extremely bad luck, they now viewed it as an experience of luminosity, as a time out of time when the gods and goddesses spoke more clearly to them of what to value and what to discard. They almost missed that heightened state of feeling. It was similar to when you've been through incredible danger with someone and whenever you see each other, you recall the nature of that experience together; you share something precious that no one else can understand. Although you wouldn't choose to go back to that experience, you might remember with some gratitude the surprising things you discovered about yourself and others: the camaraderie, generosity, and genuineness you found, qualities that seem to be lacking in the mundane, conventional world. Certainly anyone in danger—or with a broken heart— yearns for things to go back to normal. But once you are through it, you see that indeed you were actually in a state of grace, a time when the depths of human experience were yours and you stood at the nexus of hope and fear, love and loss, wholeness and dissolution. In such a situation, you find that you can actually stand right on that very spot, that you won't fall apart, and that, when you face it directly, seen and unseen angels come to your aid.

26

Authenticity

In the garden of gentle sanity,
May you be bombarded by coconuts of wakefulness.

—Chögyam Trunpga, *Timely Rain*

RECENTLY, a conversation took place on my blog about falling
in love. Two readers had had a similar experience. They had each
fallen madly, passionately in love and had their hearts broken when
their lovers had suddenly terminated the relationships. "There is
no point for wanting or desiring anything in this world," said one
of the readers about the deeply nihilistic place she found herself in
while struggling to recover. "My soul grieves for him every day,"
said the other. For each of them, someone else had come along and
they had found themselves in "nice" relationships with good, decent people. But both missed the fire and passion of being head over
heels in love. What to do? Was the kind of divine passion each had
experienced with previous lovers bound to end in despair? Was
that kind of love simply "not real"? Were relationships with sweet,
nice people the best they could hope for? One of them wrote: "I
look out onto the romantic horizon of my life with this man and I
want to take a nap."

They both left comments wondering whether it was better to
stay with "decent" partners or set out once again to find a more ecstatic kind of love and risk the horrific pain of heartbreak once
again. This is a damn good question. Here's what I said:

"The issues you both point out are so monumental and confusing. It sounds to me like the questions you're posing are along these lines: Which kind of love is the kind I should seek? Where does my heart belong? How far should I go for love?"

These are good questions, but they are unanswerable. They imply that the locus of control lies within you, that you can choose a certain person or vision of love and then go after it, or even that you can somehow dispose of the pain of heartbreak. But love just happens and the outcome can't be controlled, no matter how passionately you give yourself. You simply cannot choose between what you had once and what you have now. What you had is gone. You can't get it back. Even if that person came back on his knees, you still couldn't have what you once had. Trying to reenter love is like trying to dip your foot in the same river twice. The water is always rushing forward; and each time you step into it, it's different. Sometimes the current is rough and other times it's still. All you can do is feel what it feels like now, and now, and now. I'm not trying to say that this is all great news or anything. It's just how it is.

The issue then is how you live authentically and love authentically. How clearly and vividly and tenderly can you *be* yourself, feel what you feel? How truthfully can you acknowledge your own experience, without hope or fear? How patiently and gently can you embrace yourself as you ride the waves of passion, remorse, boredom, grief? Your willingness to live this way shows fearlessness.

Much as we all (myself included) might like to strategize about love, we can't. We can only welcome it when it appears, no matter what its form, and mourn its absence should it depart. Right now you're engaged in the only battle that matters: to keep your heart tender, soft, and alive, no matter what. Your weapons are curiosity, openness, and the willingness to feel. Accepting your experience with kindness is the best way you can support yourself, and I truly hope you will both be gentle with yourselves and those you love.

So if you are driven mad by intense yearning, don't try to quell it by drunk dialing or racing out to the gym. Let it overtake and defeat you; feel its power until it subsides. When you are touched by another's sweetness, don't try to compare it to past or future loves, simply drink in that sweetness and feel its delicate softness until it's gone. When you are confused about what and who you want, allow confusion to bounce and ping and ricochet within you until it doesn't anymore. This is a physical experience; let these things move through and take over your body, feel passion in your belly, sweetness in your chest, or confusion as carbonation throughout your nervous system—or however they manifest in your being. You can have complete faith that the more that you allow—and the less you *do* in response to what you feel—the more elegant, potent, and remarkable you will become. Really. Even if you're basically a walking wreck with your nose raw and red from crying.

Give yourself over to what you feel. Let it turn your world upside down and bounce you from here to Venus and back again. Unfettered, your feelings will always, always (eventually) return to stillness. In the meantime you will come into possession of the most magnetizing, potent quality there is: authenticity. We know when we're in the company of someone who has cut through hesitation to be brilliant, ridiculous, gentle, and natural. They evince the most compelling and authoritative quality there is. Naturalness and authenticity are being who you are and feeling what you feel from moment to moment, without judging your experience as in or out of line with who you hoped you were or read you were supposed to be. *Basta*. Enough. Just be who you are. This ultimate manifestation of confidence comes only through continuous vulnerability to your world. Give yourself over to fearlessness; it is the power of authentic presence realized.

27

The Meaning of
All These Tears

YOU CRY when you're falling asleep. You cry when you wake up. Of course you cry when he comes to get his stuff out of the house. You cry the first time you pick up the dry cleaning post-breakup because he always picked up the dry cleaning. You cry when a waitress brings you your coffee black when you asked for it with milk because he drank it black. Road signs, message T-shirts, overheard conversations, television commercials, pop songs (especially pop songs) can cause immediate code-red emotional overload and you burst into tears. Again.

One way to think of all these tears is as a flood of love. Liberated from its object, love now flows freely, powerfully, mercilessly, as rain, as sorrow, and as longing. When your heart is broken, it is broken open and in some sense your limitations in love have been removed. All the love you had for a particular person is still there, but instead of attaching to an object, it floats freely. It is groundless and without reference point.

Through one lens, this is a supremely painful situation. It is. But through another, it is something else. I won't say that this something else is pleasurable, but it is real. It is real and raw and deep, and even if you don't want it to be this way (you'd rather your love had an object), it is. And now that you're here, up to your neck with love unbound, you could try to do something with it. Because although it doesn't feel good, it is very, very precious. In fact, it is wild and deep and basically unmanageable. This is your heart. Freed of the containment of relationship, it roars. You didn't know all this energy and intensity was in there to begin with. What you thought was a cute little kitty cat, you now see has been a ferocious mountain lion all along.

Have you noticed that, in your state of heartbreak, everything touches you? And not just what happens to you personally, but what happens around you. If you're watching a movie and the lead character loses his love, you know precisely what he is feeling and you cry with him. If you walk down the street and see a child who has momentarily lost her mommy, the look on her face now tears you apart completely. Before you would have felt bad for her, sure, but you wouldn't be reduced to tears yourself. In either case, you would help her locate her mother, but now it's with a sense of emotional alignment and the fierce wish to see her suffering end, not just to do a good turn for another. And when mother and child are reunited, you have so much more than a sense of having been a good Samaritan. You rejoice with them and totally don't care if anyone thanks you or not.

This sense of emotional communion with others extends beyond spurned lovers and lost children. It now includes basically anyone who is feeling or experiencing anything genuine— and does not include anything disingenuous, whatsoever. You are no longer moved by polite expressions of happiness or sadness; you can see right through them. When someone you love suffers, you feel it so deeply and long for her to have relief. Your friends' troubles touch your heart, not just your mind. And the troubles of strangers, should you see a person on the bus with a beaten-down expression or overhear a conversation at the bank about someone's financial woes, these, too, can touch you. And you might even soften a teeny-tiny bit toward those whom you consider your "enemies," because you can imagine that just behind their ridiculous behavior is probably some kind of pain, just like you are feeling.

It's as if you've left one world of emotional give-and-take and entered another one, one that is very broad, in which everything you encounter has a tinge of rawness. In fact, you have entered another world. You stand in the doorway of the world to the bodhisattva.

"Bodhisattva" is a Sanksrit word. *Bodhi* means "awake" and *sattva* means "being." So a bodhisattva is an awakened being, someone who has awakened to the existence of others in a heightened, fundamental way. Usually we view others as potential devices for our own fulfillment or disappointment. A bodhisattva views others as discrete from her wishes or fears about them. This is a huge shift and is one way to look at what you are experiencing right now— the beginnings of this greater awareness.

Along with wakefulness and greater awareness comes, quite spontaneously, a loosening of boundaries. Your heart goes out to others much more naturally and you find a kind of attunement with the world around you. It's as though you had thought you were playing a flute all alone in your house but find that actually an orchestra accompanies you. A melodious cacophony of joy, sorrow, rage, delight, numbness, and ecstasy is playing all around you. Now you can hear it; you can feel it. You are awake. And just like any great improviser, you take it in directly and begin to play to it. Even the things and people who disturb you do so honestly and clearly. You can feel yourself respond with snootiness or agitation or negative judgment, and you know that *you* own these feelings and they're simply notes in this miraculous display of sound. The energy that a bodhisattva takes in from the world around her burns clean and leaves no mess.

So what are you going to do with all this energy that, although it contains profound meaning, basically messes up your entire world? Much as you may long to go back to a purely self-referential existence, you can't. And it's not as if you're going to become some kind of Mother Teresa overnight either, always being all "I care only for the needs of others." You're entering a new level of emotional awareness and receptivity, but you're not there yet. At first this might feel awkward, undesirable—but it's also crazily creative, meaningful, distressing, and, most of all, alive. You are alive. In this aliveness is a profound kind of grace, and, eventually, you will come to manifest it with elegance. So just hold on and let your broken heart lead you there.

28

One Sorry-Ass
Bodhisattva Wannabe

Taking the bodhisattva vow implies that instead of holding onto
our individual territory and defending it tooth and nail, we become
open to the world that we are living in.

—Chögyam Trungpa

WAKING UP and becoming a bodhisattva isn't so simple. It requires tuning in to your environment in a totally different way. Just
as with marriage, it helps to make a formal vow if you want to attempt something so improbable. Vows change your life. So far, I've
made two vows. One was when I took a formal vow to become a
bodhisattva. The other was to become a wife.

To Buddhists, a bodhisattva is a person who vows to help all
beings reach enlightenment, no matter how many lifetimes it
might take. This vow is obviously not made lightly; it comes after
many hours of meditation practice and a formal commitment to
Buddhism. Serious contemplation and study are required to get
even a glimmer of the deeper meaning of this vow and its complex-
ities. (For example, you vow to love everyone, even people you
don't like.)

A wife's vow is also not made lightly. It comes after having
found someone you really, really like to talk to and also to touch. It's
made after serious contemplation of the likelihood that you'll find

anyone better or otherwise grow old alone, and how cute you'd look in a bridal gown. A bodhisattva chooses to be of service. A bride picks out china patterns for dinner service. Oh, and also chooses to love her husband even when she doesn't like him.

It so happened that I prepared to take both these vows around the same time. While bride-me was shopping for dresses, arguing with her parents, and falling prey to panic attacks, bodhisattva-me was studying transcendent actions and contemplating the suffering of all sentient beings.

Both are vows to love (all beings in one case and a single being in the other) and it may seem that the bodhisattva vow is the really hard one. But after ten years I can tell you that the real test of big-heartedness started in being married.

When my boyfriend asked me to marry him, I didn't exactly gush yes. I sort of tried to break up with him. He wanted to deepen our relationship, and I just wasn't sure. Sure, I loved Duncan, but my divorced girlfriends had loved their boyfriends, too. Clearly love was no basis for marriage. Then what was? It had to be about more than wearing a pretty dress, waving around a wedding ring, and being all "Oh, it's my day."

I told him I needed time to think it over and wanted to spend a month apart. I planned to search my soul, ponder the question deeply, and meditate a lot. I didn't really know if I was cut out for marriage. I prized my solitude tremendously, maybe above everything. When I wanted to write, I wrote. When I wanted to meditate, I meditated. When I wanted to pretend to write and meditate, no one was around to bust me. I wasn't sure I wanted to give all this up.

Plus, without being married we could easily ignore what drove each of us crazy about the other and, perhaps as a consequence, after three years we were still completely hot for each other. Privacy. Being able to get away from each other on our bad days. These were good things, no? Maybe maintaining some separation was the key to keeping the whole thing going.

By month's end I figured I'd either come to some sort of brilliant conclusion about how it could all work out, OR that I simply wasn't built for marriage and we should break up. If the latter, I'd already have accumulated separation days and maybe they could be backdated to shorten the grieving period.

During all this, I noticed that I was crying a lot. Everything was touching me and it was getting on my nerves: the hopeful look on a colleague's face when he was about to make a presentation; how sorry I felt for the people on the news; how beautiful Marvin Gaye's voice was when he sang "What's Going On." The insulation between me and the world around me was getting thinner and thinner. So I stepped up my meditation practice. I thought this would be the best way to maintain equilibrium during this emotional time. But the more I meditated, the more likely I was to be provoked to tears by the slightest display of fragility. This couldn't be the intended result. Instead of making me peaceful, meditating was freaking me out. What was I doing wrong?

I made an appointment with my meditation instructor to explore this question, but instead of giving me a strategy for toughening up, he suggested I take the bodhisattva vow to become an awakened being. He told me the vow was something that a Buddhist might consider to deepen her practice after having been a meditator for some years. (Again with the deepening.) *Sure,* I thought, *who wouldn't want to try to become enlightened?*

But there was a catch. "The vow is to attain enlightenment for all beings, not just for yourself. You vow to keep taking birth through endless lifetimes and helping out until all beings are enlightened," he said. No exceptions. You volunteer to take on the pain of all others. *Wow, that's some vow,* I thought. But how, I asked him, would this help me stop crying all the time? It sounded like it would make everything worse. The tears are a good sign, he said. It's good preparation for the path of the bodhisattva. *Okay, if you say so,* I thought.

I spent a month weighing the pros and cons of getting married, figuring that at some point one would outweigh the other. One problem with my strategy: the more I thought it all over, the more I realized that I totally, completely loved Duncan and there was nothing I could do about it. No matter how heavy the con side of the list got with perfectly acceptable reasons not to marry (familiarity kills desire . . . all my private time will disappear . . . I can't poop when anyone else is in the house), they couldn't trump the one solitary thing on the pro side: I loved him. (Okay, and there would be tax advantages.) I didn't even know why I loved him so much. I mean, he's great and cute and funny and all that, but nothing could account for the pleasure I got from his breath on my shoulder as we fell asleep or how upsetting I found it when anyone was mean to him.

When we got back together after our month apart, I told him how much I loved him and gave him a carefully thought-out list of caveats: I'd never be a conventional wife. I'd require time and space to meditate every day. Please don't talk to me when I'm in the bathroom. And so on. In the midst of my big presentation, he reached into his backpack and retrieved a small package. *Oh no,* I thought, *does he think that giving me a ring will wash away all doubts and common sense?*

But there was no ring. Instead, he handed me a little heart-shaped box. Inside was a backyard bird feather and a smooth white stone. "This is us," he said. "I'm the rock and you're the feather. Fly all you want. That's just who you are. I'll make our situation stable. That's who I am."

I was flabbergasted. What? He saw me this clearly and still wanted to marry me? The gravity of my rules and conditions shifted as suddenly as a flock of birds in the sky. I burst into tears. I had no idea there could be a person as wonderful as him. At this point there was no choice. "Yes," I said. "Yes, yes, yes. Please marry me and I will marry you."

So we began to plan our wedding. I placed the sweet box with the rock and the feather by my bed so I could look at it any time I wanted. Whenever we would have a fight or my doubts would return, I could lift the top and peek inside. *Oh yes,* I would remind myself, *everything is okay. We love each other so much.*

During this month I was also studying in preparation for the bodhisattva vow ceremony. I read about how great saints and scholars defined compassion and how they kept it going even under the most difficult circumstances. I learned that compassion is the sole basis for peace and that personal happiness can come only from making the needs of others primary. I once read that the Dalai

Lama spends three hours every morning rousing compassion, but I have no idea how he then goes out into the world without sobbing all the time. But just as with marrying Duncan, after thinking about the awakening vow, I realized I had to do it. I simply had no choice. Do you say no when the one you love offers to love you back for the rest of his life? Do you say no when your meditation teacher asks if you want to try to become enlightened for the benefit of others? "Actually, I think I'd rather remain in a self-absorbed fantasy" isn't a good answer to either of them. So I said yes. Okay, yes, yes, yes. I'll try.

Within a few months I took the bodhisattva vow with about ten other students. We had been told to bring something to place on the altar as an offering during the ceremony. It didn't have to be the most meaningful thing in our lives, but it should be something that mattered. I thought about offering a ring that I rarely wore, or books that had been very meaningful to me, or even my favorite dress. (Look, I really loved that dress.) None of them seemed right. There was only one thing that would cost me to be without—the box with the rock and the feather. I tried to talk myself out of it. "He said it didn't have to be our most valued possession." "That would hurt Duncan." "Surely I could hold on to this. . . ."

I didn't know if I was making a generous gesture or a martyred one when I offered the box during the vow ceremony. But I did it anyway.

The very next morning I woke up in a panic. I was bereft. I wanted that box back. I had never possessed anything so precious. But it was gone and nothing, nothing, nothing could bring it back. Even if I could find it and return it to my bedside table, now it would be only a sad reminder of how selfish I was, not how beloved. I was stuck. I saw just how unlikely a candidate for bodhisattva-hood I was. I couldn't even graciously give up a cardboard box for the benefit of others, to say nothing of my "personal space" for my boyfriend. Could I change my mind about these vows, or was it too late?

Too late. I had already gotten my first lesson. You can't give to get. Opening yourself to another isn't as simple as acting nice or giving up what you value even though you really, really don't want to. It's actually heartbreaking. I knew I had no idea how to be a bodhisattva—or a wife, for that matter. Nor could I pretend these were stupid ideas and go back to living the way I had before. Anything I gained for myself alone would be a reminder of my lack of loving-kindness. I couldn't be bodhisattva Susan but I couldn't be regular Susan either. Bastards! I was trapped. So, of course, I burst into tears.

Instead of making it safe, love—whether for all beings or for one—actually breaks your heart. Being loved is uncomfortable; and the more I love, the more uncomfortable it is. In the end, I'm still not quite sure what I've vowed to do either as a wife or a bodhisattva, except to break my own heart, over and over. And to see what happens next.

So, as you make your way through heartbreak and begin to contemplate a new relationship (and odds are, you will), please keep in mind that what you are experiencing now prepares you to love more truly. A broken heart teaches you to open up to someone else and see him for who he is, not just who you wish he were. It acquaints you with your own vulnerability as a source of strength, not weakness. When you do fall in love, you will understand much more clearly how precious this love is, how tenuous, and how profound. You will appreciate it so deeply, and at the same time be able to accommodate love's uncertainty.

Whomever you decide to give your heart to will be very lucky to have found one such as you, a person who has learned how to love.

29

Tears and Awakening

LAST SUMMER I attended a month-long meditation retreat. We practiced meditation for as much as six or seven hours a day punctuated by occasional dharma talks from a meditation instructor. Every few days our teacher himself would come to discuss an aspect of spiritual view or practice and then we had a question-and-answer session. One day he gave a particularly incisive, inspiring talk on the importance of cultivating genuine compassion, which is so much more than just being all nice all the time. When you realize the nature of compassion, he said, you realize the nature of reality. You become enlightened. It was time for us—his senior students—to really go for it and devote ourselves to becoming enlightened for the benefit of all beings. He discussed details of how to cultivate compassion and pitfalls we might look out for.

I had already spent some years working on developing compassion, but I seemed to run into the same snag over and over—an inability to open myself to the suffering of others without just falling apart and either dissolving into tears or pretending I wasn't about to. When I practiced opening myself to my own suffering and the suffering of others, at a certain point it would become unbearable and all I could do was cry. When I thought of the people on the news or the fact of my parents' aging, or just the everyday suffering we all experience (losing lovers, failing at work, etc.), I couldn't help it, I would just sob.

When it was time for questions, I decided I had to ask him if sobbing uncontrollably has a role in cultivating compassion. It just felt so destabilizing. Surely this couldn't be what the Buddha was recommending as the path to enlightenment or a helpful gift I could offer others. When it came to empathy and care for my fellow humans, wiping my nose on their sleeves did not seem like the best thing I could offer them. But then what?

When I got up to go to the mic and ask my teacher this question, I could feel these very same tears stinging behind my eyeballs. *Oh no,* I thought, *I'm going to cry when I ask him about crying. This is awful. But I have to do it.* "Sir," I said, "when I attempt to rouse compassion by acknowledging suffering, the more I let in the truth of suffering, the more likely I am to collapse in tears. Surely this isn't the intended result. How can I move past this?" He looked at me with such kindness and said, "You know, some of the world's greatest meditators have cried a lot."

I've been thinking about his answer ever since. I've been conjuring images of the world's meditation masters and sages, such as the Buddha, Jesus, and Gandhi, and trying to picture them, not as implacable adepts who always knew what to do and say, but as human beings who cried—under the Bodhi Tree, atop the Mount of Olives, in a prison cell—for all of us. But then what? They didn't just wipe their eyes and return to their lives, hoping for the best. They gained something from their tears. They learned something from them. They weren't reduced to a weakened condition; they were made stronger by their tears and were left with a greater capacity for love, not less.

As you recognize and admit your own strong emotions, you give yourself more inner space to accommodate them. You don't center on getting rid of pain and creating a situation where you'll never feel such pain again. (Much as you might wish never to feel it again.) Instead, you let these deep, painful emotions create the perfect circumstances for you to become a more truthful version of who you already are. One thing is guaranteed to arise from this self-discovery: enduring happiness. It is a wonderful truth that, buried in the muck and mire of that most devastating of emotional difficulties, a broken heart, is the possibility of freedom from suffering.

30

The Practice of Loving-Kindness

I WANT TO INTRODUCE YOU to the meditation practice of Loving-Kindness. This meditation teaches you how to rouse and offer the love in your heart, no matter how bent out of shape you are. You may come to see that, when feeling unloved, the act of offering love actually helps more than trying to get love. I don't know why. It just works that way. Loving-Kindness shows you how to offer your love on the spot, no matter how torn up you feel, and to anyone at all, even people you hate. There is awesome power in choosing to offer love genuinely. It can't be a fake nicey-nice endeavor, but a true outpouring of the heart.

Learning that you have an endless supply of love in your heart and that no amount of relationship woe can ever quench that flame is tremendously empowering. But love isn't only an emotion, it is also an activity. You can choose to engage in it as often as you wish. The more you understand love, the more skillfully you can love, and Loving-Kindness Meditation is a practice designed to acquaint you more fully with this activity. It turns out that offering love is the key to recovering from having lost love.

The story of Loving-Kindness Meditation begins with the Buddha himself, over 2,500 years ago. He had directed a group of monks to do a retreat in a forest, but when they tried to meditate, the creatures of the forest felt bothered. They tried to drive out the monks by making lots of scary noises and creating an awful stench. It worked. The monks couldn't concentrate on their meditation and so decided to return to the Buddha and request a less noisy, less stinky spot. Apparently, all the forests were full up and so instead of redirecting them, the Buddha gave them the practice of Loving-Kindness Meditation and sent them back to their original spot.

So they returned, and instead of trying to ignore the forest creatures in order to focus on their meditation, they opened their hearts and minds to these creatures and wished them well. They imagined the distress they were causing as a bunch of strangers who had unexpectedly taken up residence in the creatures' home, so instead of wishing they'd go away, the monks felt sad for the forest dwellers. From their hearts, they concentrated on sending happiness and ease to the inhabitants of the forest.

It worked. As the story goes, the creatures felt so loved that instead of pelting the monks with stink bombs, they undertook to protect the monks and guard their meditation spots. They not only made room for the monks, they softened toward them in return and completely loved them back. This is the magic of Loving-Kindness. Time-tested and trustworthy, it creates remarkable softness in both practitioner and recipient.

This practice of Loving-Kindness involves rousing the loving-kindness you already possess and then offering it (I'll explain how) to yourself, then to a loved one, a stranger, an enemy, and, finally, to all beings everywhere. You make the offering with certain phrases that you say silently to yourself (also explained below).

When I learned this practice, I was surprised that it started with offering loving-kindness to myself. I thought this was supposed to be about loving others. Well, it turns out that by first connecting with your own search for love and the joys and sorrows that have resulted, you can more easily empathize with others searching for the same thing. You can assume that what you feel, they feel, too, albeit in their own way. Underneath, their yearnings are the same as yours. As much as you wish for love for yourself, you can also wish for it for these other people. It's not a huge leap, but at the same time it's a very big step in healing and opening your heart.

Here is instruction in the practice. You can also find guided audio instruction at my website at susanpiver.com/meditation _instruction.

It is always good to begin with a few minutes of Tranquility practice to make your mind a bit more peaceful. So if you can, please do so. Sit on a chair or cushion and focus your attention on your breath for a few cycles or until you feel settled. Then for Loving-Kindness practice, you can remain sitting or lie down. Basically, arrange yourself in a comfortable position. Close your eyes.

Now, with your eyes closed, bring to mind something that is currently causing you sorrow, anger, disappointment, or any sort of emotional distress. It could be a general sense of the heartbreak you're currently experiencing or it could be a specific aspect of it— for example, you're sad because tonight you're going to a party alone. Or it could be something entirely different: your wish to be closer to your mother, a financial worry, or even being upset about your weight or age. (Hey, sorrows of vanity are no less painful than other kinds!) Whatever it is, key in on this distressing feeling. Note how sad, agitated, hopeless, or whatever else it makes you feel. If you start to cry, it's okay. Once you have identified a particular strain of sorrow, connect with how it reflects your search for happiness and how, in this case, that search failed. The important thing here is to connect, not with that sense of failure, but with the yearning and sweetness that underlie your search. You're simply trying to find happiness, and you can honor this by wishing yourself the following:

> *May I be happy.*
> *May I be healthy.*
> *May I be peaceful.*
> *May I live with ease.*

These are the sorts of phrases that are used traditionally, and they are certainly excellent. If you like, however, you can choose words that are more resonant for you—but, if you do, definitely keep it very simple. ("May I be happy and Paul, too, but may Suzy and Biff be miserable," for example, is not a good phrase.)

When I'm heartbroken, these are the ones I choose. They're only slightly different from the traditional phrases.

> *May I be happy.*
> *May I be healthy.*
> *May I be seen and fully embraced.*
> *May I know the joy of love.*

These phrases connect me with my own personal desires, especially number three, which reflects the wish to be seen for who I am. This is my particular yearning. You might choose something like, "May I be appreciated for all I do," or "May I find self-respect," or "May I be free of fear." These are all good.

For the purpose of explaining this exercise, I'm going to stick with the traditional phrases. So, still sitting with your eyes closed and holding a sense of your personal struggles for happiness, send the following wishes to yourself:

> *May I be happy.*
> *May I be healthy.*
> *May I be peaceful.*
> *May I live with ease.*

Repeat these silently to yourself for as long as you like, which could be just saying them three times or spending two or ten minutes absorbed in asking for these things for yourself.

When you are ready, we'll move on to the next stage, which is sending loving-kindness to someone you love. Choose a person who makes love effortlessly blossom in your heart when you think of them. You don't have to try at all. It could be a child, a parent or sibling, a dear friend, a prized teacher, or even a pet. If you cannot think of anyone you know, think of a historic or public figure whom you admire. Once you find this person, fix his or her image in your mind. As best you can, see his or her face. When you have conjured a sense of this person's presence, acknowledge all that he does to find happiness, whether or not you know the details. This loved one has worked so hard, and you may know of particular triumphs or disappointments he has met with. Send him the same phrases you sent to yourself.

> *May you be happy.*
> *May you be healthy.*
> *May you be peaceful.*
> *May you live with ease.*

Again, spend as much time as you like working the open stream of loving-kindness that flows from your heart into the other person's.

When you are done, let this loved one's face or image go. The next phase of the practice is about offering loving-kindness to a stranger, what is traditionally called "the neutral person." This means someone whom you encounter fairly regularly, but about whom you have no particular feelings, positive or negative. It could be the woman who sells you coffee every morning, the man you walk by on the way to the train, or a colleague or classmate who sits a few desks away but with whom you rarely interact. As best you can, fix this person's face in your mind.

At this point, in addition to being meaningful, the practice starts to become very interesting. Who knew you could love a stranger? Well, you can, as we're about to see. You can assume that, just like you and your loved one, this person has had his or her own struggles on the path to happiness. In her search, she has met with hopes, fears, shock, disappointment, and surprising obstacles. Even if she seems the most chipper or wholesome person in the world, you can bet that this is true. Holding her in mind, send her the wishes.

> *May you be happy.*
> *May you be healthy.*
> *May you be peaceful.*
> *May you live with ease.*

Sharon Salzberg, a Buddhist teacher who is known worldwide for the profundity of her teachings on loving-kindness, tells about a loving-kindness retreat she did in Southeast Asia for several months. Each participant chose one person for each category and stuck with that person for the entire retreat. For her neutral person, she had chosen an Asian man whom she encountered every day but did not interact much with. Unbeknownst to him, she had been practicing sending him loving-kindness for lengthy periods, every single day. As she practiced, this person, whom she had seen as rather two-dimensional, began to fill out and actually become quite dear to her. She felt more and more tenderness toward him as the retreat progressed, and it was like her sweet secret. I love that story. It shows so clearly how, by simply opening your heart to anyone, even a stranger, you can develop a sense of softness toward him or her.

The next, and second to last, phase of the practice is where it gets *really* interesting. The person to whom you will next send loving-kindness is traditionally called "the enemy." This is someone who has done you wrong. Someone who has hurt you, offended you, disappointed you, or enraged you. It's probably best not to choose the person you revile most in this world, although if you choose to, it's fine. It may be easier, however, to begin with someone who has hurt you more mildly. It can be someone from the present or the past. If you can't think of anyone, you could choose a historical or public figure you find particularly repulsive. In any case, it should be someone who you definitely do not like.

Bring this person's face, image, or just the sense of his presence to mind. Underneath that person's efforts and machinations is also the simple wish to be happy. Just like you, your loved one, and the stranger, this person is trying in his or her own weird way to be happy. It may look totally asinine or worse to you, but still, this is the motivation. This is simply how all beings are built. Taking this into account, you can send the enemy the wishes.

May you be happy.
May you be healthy.
May you be peaceful.
May you live with ease.

When I do this practice, I tend to shortchange or overdo it with the enemy. I either spend less time on him or her because I just don't like him or her, or more time because I feel guilty about my puny likes and dislikes. Try to be evenhanded. Don't under- or overdo it. Spend about as much time on your enemy as you have with the others. Of course, if you find yourself needing to do otherwise, go right ahead.

The final stage of the practice is to let go of this enemy and rouse the idea that just like all the people you've just considered, all beings everywhere—human, animal, insect, known to you or unknown; of the past, present, or future—are simply searching for security for themselves and their kin. Just like you, they are striving for happiness, health, peace, and ease. You can totally identify with this. From this point of sympathy, send the wishes that all beings everywhere will also find happiness. Have a sense that your wishes extend out from your heart center, in front of you and behind, above you and below, and in all directions. Like a giant disco ball spinning slowly in your heart center, your love radiates sparkly, soft beams of prismatic light that can circle the globe, sometimes touching down softly and sometimes flashing a surprising shock of light.

To close the practice, simply let it go completely. Stop practicing Loving-Kindness. Open your eyes and rest in the space of non-effort for a few minutes or as long as you like. Rise with conviction in your own and others' basic goodness.

31

Loving-Kindness Meditation and the One Who Broke Your Heart

OKAY, welcome to big-girl territory. I'm going to suggest that the most potent step you can take toward your own healing is to extend loving-kindness to your ex. It doesn't matter how thoroughly unlikely and distasteful this may seem. It doesn't matter if you think it's hypocritical because you'd be totally faking. In fact, the more impossible it seems, the more impact the practice will have. And P.S., it's okay to pretend at first. It doesn't matter if it's too scary to do this because you still love him so much you're afraid to reopen yourself to feelings of affection. In all of these cases, the practice of Loving-Kindness will bring a feeling of stability and peace to your inner world.

As we've seen from the practice of Loving-Kindness so far, it is possible to extend your heart to people you have no intention of loving, including strangers and enemies. You don't have to like them or approve of them to do so; you just have to slow down, admit to your own sorrow, and watch as, quite naturally, judgment and anger toward others dissolve into loving-kindness. You're wired that way; it's totally natural. We've all had the experience of seemingly solid emotions such as anger, righteousness, or pity turn to something much softer once your perspective expands.

Think of a time that a colleague pissed you off by showing up for a department meeting unprepared and cranky. You may have harbored thoughts about her incompetence and selfishness—until another coworker told you that she was taking care of a parent who had suddenly fallen ill. In a flash, without thinking about it, you imagine how you would feel if a loved one experienced unpredictable health problems and, boom, instead of plotting revenge, you're plotting a department lunch to cheer her up. Or perhaps you recently learned that your neighbors' dog had to be put down and even though you've never even spoken to this family, every time you pass their house, you feel sad for them. You remember how you felt when this happened to you. Enemies and strangers can become friends with one little flick of some internal switch. A single thought can make this happen, and it's not at all phony. Your heart is built to blossom open at the slightest provocation, and although it can feel a little uncomfortable, it is also extremely earthy and real. In fact, it can change the world. This is a very important principle. And in any case, feeling kindly toward others is just way less exhausting than judgmentalism, apathy, and irritation.

I'm not asking you to find a way to soften toward your ex, not at all. You don't have to forgive, forget, or like him to experience loving-kindness for him. I'm simply asking you to try including him in your Loving-Kindness practice and see what happens. I've heard all sorts of stories from people who have done this practice for those they simply don't like, or even hate. Most find that their own hatred loosens its grip on their souls and it feels as though a poison is being drained. It's not unusual to find that within days or weeks of regularly sending genuine loving-kindness to someone with whom you have a seemingly intractable problem, some kind of shift occurs: you are no longer quite so angry, you receive a note of apology, you run into someone having the same difficulty and a friendship begins. In any case, whether due to a shift in your mind or in your external circumstances, this practice delivers relief.

The key word here: *genuine.* If you perform this practice to invoke a result beyond the stated blessing or with a hidden agenda, it is no longer genuine and loses its mojo. So keep the practice simple, grounded, and intimately connected to the contents of your heart.

To begin, find a comfortable place to sit or lie down, where you won't be disturbed. As before, begin the practice of Loving-Kindness Meditation with yourself. Bring your attention to your heart, your actual physical heart. Notice how it feels. Is your heart constricted, heavy, numb, or something else? As you allow awareness to settle there, touch in with your experience of loss and the impact it has had on you, as epitomized by the sensations around your heart or wherever else you may notice your sorrow reflected. Please wish yourself well by offering yourself the phrases *May I be happy, May I be healthy, May I be peaceful, May I live with ease* (or whatever other simple phrases may seem appropriate). Notice what you feel you have lost and how deep your longing for love is, whether from this person or someone else.

When you feel that you have sufficiently wished yourself well, bring your ex up in your mind. Get a sense of him by visualizing his face or feeling his presence. Know that, no matter how insanely unreasonable or subtly off base his actions have been, he, too, has the very same longing as you. He simply wants to find love and be happy. Regardless of your feelings about how he goes about securing these things, you can wish that he find them. Simply offer him the same phrases.

When you are finished, let the practice of Loving-Kindness go and rest in simple breath awareness for a few minutes or as long as you like.

You can do this practice on the spot, and in very creative ways. You can flash loving-kindness to your ex when you're driving in the car or sitting in class. You can flash it to yourself, too. If you're walking down the street and see a couple arguing, you can offer them loving-kindness as you walk by. If you see a movie or hear a song that seems to describe your relationship, you can offer loving-kindness to the characters or musicians. Anytime you detect a hint out there in the world of what you are experiencing, take it in, identify with it, imagine what this other person may be feeling, and offer your heart. Embedded in this moment, this particular action, this slight turn of mind, is the power to heal all sorrows.

32

Turning Off the Projector

WHEN I WAS THINKING of getting married, I was terrified. I felt that I had already had my heart broken in enough love affairs and realized that those heartbreaks would be nothing compared to the broken heart that could result from a failed marriage. I mean, losing the person you hang out with all the time is one thing, but losing the one with whom you've publicly and privately proclaimed the intention to build a life with—and failed—was another altogether. The stakes were so high.

During the time I took away from him before we got married, I gave a lot of thought to heartbreak and to why my past relationships had failed. With a few notable exceptions, they hadn't failed because we had stopped loving each other. They had failed because someone, usually I, didn't love our life together. It had nothing to do with whether or not he was as cute, smart, funny, and sweet as I had thought in the beginning of our relationship and more to do with whether or not we liked each other's friends, how he treated his parents, or what kind of house we wanted. Those kinds of things. I had an epiphany that at the time was a real eye-opener: *Just because you love someone, it doesn't mean you're going to love your life together.*

What did I know about how my boyfriend viewed our life? On

one hand, I knew everything about him. We were so intimate, and I knew his mind and body almost as well as I knew my own, or even better in some ways. But on the other hand, I had no idea about stuff such as: How much debt did he have? Would we keep our money in the same bank account? What would his son call me? Did he expect me to celebrate Christmas? And what would happen if I felt like going on a meditation retreat for a month? I guessed the answers would be—not much, no, Susan, no, and nothing. But then I realized these were my assumptions. And you know what they say about assumptions. So I wrote these and other questions down. (By the way, these questions became the basis of my first book: *The Hard Questions: 100 Essential Questions to Ask Before You Say "I Do."*)

Boy, was I in for some surprises. While I was correct in assuming that he didn't have any debt and he agreed his son should call me Susan, his other answers caught me off guard. For example, he was appalled to think I would want to keep our money in separate accounts. (Me: But I have my own business and plus, believe me, you do *not* want to know how much I spend on highlights. Him: How far are you going to take this? Will we each have our own milk carton in the fridge? Are you really in this marriage or not?) And although he didn't expect me to suddenly take up caroling, he did hope I would join him in his Christmas customs of exchanging presents, cooking a big meal, and decorating a tree. How that was different from celebrating Christmas, I wasn't sure. And as far as going away by myself for a month, I thought he knew how important my meditation practice was to me and, if anything, he would cheer me on in my efforts to deepen that practice. Au contraire. His face went white at the thought of me going away for a month with no communication between us.

I learned some important things here, and I learned them fast. First, neither of us was right or wrong in what we hoped for; the only wrong thing we could do was not acknowledge the other's wishes as legitimate. Second, and most germane for our conversation, I learned how deeply held my projections were about what my partner "should" look like and, in some cases, just how unlike those projections this real person was. At this moment, I saw that I had a choice. I could insist that he get into character with my projected ideal partner, or I could drop it all and try to love this actual human being instead. I'm sad to say, it was not an easy choice. I loved my projection boyfriend so much. However, he was a made-up guy and in front of me was a real guy, who was incredibly wonderful. So I decided to give it a try and, boom, surprise number two. Once we both recognized that each was willing to let the other off the hook for being an ideal mate and instead to love each other as we were, his hotness factor went off the charts. Perhaps mine did as well, if I may say. What I thought was already a deep love gave way to something way more precious, beautiful, and rare: loving an actual person and being loved by him for who I was. Okay, so that's a good reason to get married and we did.

Whether we're aware of it or not, we each walk through the world with a projector between our ears, and it's constantly running a film of what life is supposed to look like and how people, including ourselves, are supposed to act. Our eyes are like two lenses, and wherever we look, we project our movie out and what we see becomes part of it. We move through our experiences like actors playing roles and we seek, not other people to love, but those whom we can most easily cast as friends, colleagues, and lovers. Without awareness, we use others as plot devices. This can't go on indefinitely, and at some point the jig will be up and all will be revealed as playacting. This isn't very hospitable, when you get right down to it. And in a situation such as when you say, "I love you," to whom are you saying it? To the person in front of you or your projection onto him?

Often—very, very often—heartbreak occurs, not because love itself dies, but because our projection onto the other fails, or what is being projected onto us fails. Unlike the darkly beautiful reality of love dying, a dying projection creates urgent anxiety and emotional chaos. It's not necessarily losing the other person that hurts so badly: it's losing a made-up vision of safety. Real love, deep love, intimate love has nothing to do with security. It is wild and painful and powerful and unpredictable. Projections, however, have everything to do with the search for safety; and when this kind of love is lost, it quite understandably leaves you feeling unprotected, in a state of turmoil. Learning to discriminate between projection and reality, moment to moment, is the very important beginning of genuine wisdom. Heartbreak itself releases this wisdom like a bird from a cage.

Wisdom is not simply knowing how to avoid casting others in your drama, it is learning how to turn off the projector altogether. This is the ultimate, the finest, the deepest, and, truly, the *only* way to love fully. When you learn to give love in this way, freely and genuinely, the love that comes back to you will enter you into a field of passion that is vaster than you could ever imagine. It has no end. Each time you think you have come to the edge of that field, the imagined boundary will give way to another aspect of love that is so much sweeter and richer and, yes, heartbreaking, than you ever deemed possible. This loving without projection, loving another for whom they are and—unbearably sweet—being loved for who you really are, is what we all search for. It is true. It is indestructible. It is the love that can never be lost. Heartbreak and the self-examination that comes with it prepare you to give and receive love in this way.

Part Four

From Brokenhearted to Wholehearted

Learning to Breathe Again— A Seven-Day Program

33

The Seven-Day Rescue & Relief Program

It's been a long, a long time coming, but I know that a change is gonna come.

—Sam Cooke, "A Change Is Gonna Come"

WHEN IT COMES to a broken heart, the only way out is in. There is no way to fool the pain; it persists in the face of you trying to reason it away and your determination to move forward. This brief (seven-day, Friday-to-Friday) program is a way for you to begin to make friends with your broken heart, to move toward it rather than distance yourself from it. Although facing your broken heart can feel uncomfortable at first, this is actually the way to regain balance and draw wisdom from it instead of letting it defeat you.

When I was struggling with a broken heart, I worked every strategy known to man to get the pain to stop. I tried a lot of things that didn't help: getting drunk, using affirmations such as "I'm fine, I'm fine, I'm fine" when I was not, not, not, and throwing myself into work. I devoured every women's magazine article that listed five ways to get over a broken heart or seven ways to move on for good—but advice like "keep busy," "pamper yourself," "make a list of all the things you disliked about him," "avoid negative thoughts," and the ridiculous "have a good cry every now and then" just did not cut it. "Keep busy" turned into "clean out your closets while pretending to be insane." Pampering myself turned me into a dipsomaniac with too many new clothes that I thought might tempt him back. Listing his bad qualities only reminded me of all his good ones. Pretending I could control my misery by putting icky thoughts aside was unbelievably claustrophobic and, ultimately, a lie. And have a good cry every now and then? How about every now *and* every then?

All of this "advice" made me feel as if I should have a nice, neat system for handling my big emotions until they turned into trained pets on a leash. Uh, no. The ladies in the magazine articles may have been burning the midnight oil at the office while wearing the perfect blouse and pencil skirt, dabbing every now and then at their eyes with a monogrammed hankie, but I was channel surfing on the couch in my house at four in the morning, wearing sweatpants and a bra, blowing my nose into a paper towel because I'd burned through all the tissues long ago.

It seemed that no one was writing anything that could tell someone like me what to do. So I'm going to share with you what I did instead of following others' advice. After a lot of hit-and-miss efforts, I figured out a daily routine for myself that enabled me to start to feel normal again. I'm going to suggest that you try this routine yourself for one week. If at the end of that week you've found none of this helpful, abandon ship. Whatever you have found helpful, please keep doing.

Instead of trying to distract myself through busy-ness, self-indulgence, or wacky affirmations that were more wishful than positive thinking, I allowed my feelings to be simply as they were, at which point they began to lead me down a path to lasting insight. My broken heart became my greatest spiritual teacher, and I emerged from my little experiment a way stronger person who was both more vulnerable to love and less afraid of it at the same time.

All the things I'm going to suggest to you are things I still do, even though my heart is no longer broken—I've found them to be that beneficial. And since becoming a Buddhist meditation teacher, I've learned many more ways to meet my feelings head on and turn even the nastiest ones into wisdom, so I've included some of them, too.

The program will be fairly intensive over the weekend and is then designed so that you will be able to fit it into your work schedule. If you've purchased the book on a Tuesday and don't want to wait until Friday, please begin immediately if your schedule allows. However, it might be most beneficial for you to wait until a weekend to start and instead spend the intervening days learning to practice meditation. The more prior experience you have with the practice, the easier it will be to slip right into it.

The program will help you on two levels: it will immediately address the out-of-control, speedy thoughts that accompany heartbreak and, more slowly, it will begin to pacify your heart and help you feel more in control. Heartbreak tends to relentlessly amp up your thought processes (and subsequent actions). It's easy to become so freaked out that your mind comes up with strategy after strategy to quell the pain you're feeling: you should hate him; you should hate yourself; he's incapable of love and doesn't deserve you; it's critical that you speak right away; it's critical that you never, ever speak to him again; the solution is to start a massive weight loss program; quit your job; move to a new town; get him fired; throw out all his stuff—and on and on and on. . . . All this speed leads to even more speed until you're throwing everything you've got at this problem but, like tossing pebbles against a tidal wave, nothing actually stems the flow.

Instead of further complicating matters with further complicated strategies, our program begins on a weekend by releasing all strategies, quieting the situation down, and simplifying your mental environment.

The program begins on a Friday night after work. You spend the weekend very, very simply: practicing meditation, doing the suggested journaling exercises, perhaps taking walks, and cutting way down on TV, email, Facebook—wherever you spend most of your time. These activities are meant to help you slow down and focus on your heart, to get to know it, and begin to listen to it.

On the following days, Monday through Friday, you will introduce some everyday life activities that will further pacify emotional turmoil, including meditation and journaling exercises. On the final day you will conduct a simple ceremony to release this person from your life. By the end of this week you will have begun to let go and move forward, with kindness toward yourself and him. After all, until some kindness is included, you haven't moved on.

So without further ado, please have a look at the tools you'll use during this program. My website has additional audio instruction and also examples of how to put these tools into play. Visit susan piver.com/WOBH_program.

1. *Meditation.* This is the cornerstone of the program and for working with heartbreak as a path to wisdom. You won't be meditating *on* anything and there are no visualizations or affirmations—the meditation practice I suggest is called the Practice of Tranquility, the simple breath-awareness practice explained in chapter 8. Appendix B has condensed instruction that you can and should review before each practice session, just to refresh your memory.

2. *Journaling.* When I was heartbroken, I wrote three longhand pages in my journal every morning. I still do this. This kind of writing is sometimes called "free writing" or "morning pages," the phrase coined by Julia Cameron in her wonderful book *The Artist's Way.* You will be practicing this every day of the program, writing three pages of stream-of-consciousness writing. You just pick up a pen and paper (best not to use the computer for this) and write down whatever comes to mind, as it comes to mind. Don't censor, edit, or revise. You never have to read these words again and it totally doesn't matter if they make sense, are brilliant, profane, whiny, or mundane. Whatever they are, they are. When you're done writing, put the pages away.

3. *Writing the story.* Writing a story is different from journaling. I'm going to suggest that you write the story of your relationship—but from a third-person perspective. From the day you met until the day you parted, what would the story be if you were writing it as if it happened to someone else? I'll make more detailed suggestions for how to do this below.

4. *Loving-Kindness meditation.* As mentioned earlier in the book, Loving-Kindness meditation is about connecting with what is most painful in your life and simply wishing yourself well—and then expanding that in a wish for relief for all who suffer from what is causing you pain. It's very intimate and extremely powerful. During this program we're going to practice traditional Loving-Kindness, but with some suggested tweaks that are meant to soothe a heart that feels bereft of love. Near the end of the program, you're going to practice Loving-Kindness for the one who broke your heart. I suggest that this is the most healing exercise you can possibly do.

Preparation

During this week you will invite your broken heart to show itself as a step toward healing and strengthening. However, it would be very easy for this to turn into a pity party rather than an act of empowerment. The former is pure self-indulgence while the latter is a sacred and soulful act. How can you figure out which one you're doing?

There are three steps that you can take to make any endeavor a sacred act. They are: making offerings, requesting blessings, and dedicating the merit. Let's look at each of these three steps and then review how to employ all three to create a week of introspection and healing.

Make Offerings

An offering is something you make out of respect. Our world does not actually teach us how to act respectfully. When we're told "Respect your teacher" or "You're not respecting me, young lady," these things usually mean "Do what I say because I'm bigger and tougher than you." This kind of respect is often tinged with fear and resentment, but that's not the kind of respect we're talking about here. True respect spontaneously arises in the presence of something greater than yourself. You don't have to try to feel it, and it would feel wrong not to act respectfully, like showing up on your wedding day in regular clothes or leaving your baby's name up to chance. Some important moments command respect automatically and you don't have to figure out why. Your broken heart should be treated with respect.

You can make offerings on several levels.

Outer Offerings. Objects that are traditionally used in making offerings, no matter what the wisdom tradition, tend to center around the senses: things you can see, smell, taste, touch, or hear. Images of respected figures, flowers or scented candles, sweets, beautiful fabrics, and music are often included in sacred spaces because they are lovely and pleasing. A shrine or altar is a way of focusing the energy of these offerings, so a table covered in brocade holding a candle and a photograph is a very simple way of showcasing your offerings. It's not important to make your altar table the most beautiful in the history of the world. It is important that it be neat, clean, and show sincerity. So to begin this program, please create such an altar in your home.

Inner Offerings. Besides the outer process of placing some pretty objects on a table, making offerings also has to come from within. An inner offering comes about when you make a genuine connection with yourself. It isn't so much about whom you're making an offering to. It's not necessary to decide if you're offering to God, Buddha, your higher self, the powers of good, or what have you. This is not required. What is necessary is to get in touch with exactly who and what you are right at this moment and offer that. Anything else is too abstract.

For example, as I write this, I notice that on this particular morning, I am actually quite agitated. I'm not sure I know how to say what I want to say. I notice myself becoming frustrated and then despairing. Okay. No problem. Today, what I offer is my agitation, frustration, and despair. It feels good to do this. On other days I might offer my excitement, gratitude, or joy.

The way to make an inner offering is to feel your feelings as accurately as you can and then say quite simply to yourself, "I have no idea how it will happen, but I offer it for the benefit of myself and all beings." And then let it go. I've made offerings in this way countless times (I offer my crankiness. I offer my pettiness. I offer my self-judgment. I offer my sneezes, tears, and longings for cupcakes.) I've offered my emotions. (I offer my neediness. I offer my anger at my husband. On other days I offer the love I feel for him.) I've offered the very best of who I am, on those days when I feel those things. (I offer my insights, tenderness, and deep goodness.) You can offer your whole heart. You can offer your broken heart, so that it may be used to benefit all. So when you make an offering as part of a spiritual practice, be sure to connect in with who you are right now.

Secret Offerings. As you can see from the examples above, it's not difficult to imagine making an offering from an outer or an inner perspective. The secret level is something else. It's secret from you, too, which makes it kind of exciting and interesting.

We all know what it is to make a gesture (say, send a friend in the hospital flowers) and understand the outer reason (she's sick and needs cheering up) and the inner reason (you love her). The secret reason, however, is not known to you, and that's why it's called secret. In this case, it may be that your friend was about to give up hope until the moment your flowers arrived and she was inspired to get healthy. You had no way of knowing what her feelings were or planning for your gift to arrive at the exact right moment. It just did. Other forces are at work, and for this we can be grateful. So when it comes to offerings, the way to make your secret offering (in addition to the outer and inner offerings) is to do the only thing you can do when it comes to secrets: not know them. Let go of your outer and inner offerings and agree not to trap them by your own expectation of outcome. I offer these flowers (good) because my heart is broken (good) and I want Johnny to come back (bad).

Please offer flowers. Please do so because your heart is broken. But leave the outcome up to the gods. Let the secret remain a secret.

Request Blessings

Requesting blessings, as with secret offerings, requires you to give up knowing what a blessing looks like exactly. Requesting what *you* think will make you happy (bring Johnny back to me) is like making a reservation at a five-star restaurant and then asking if you can go back into the kitchen and cook your own meal. Why go out? Instead of cooking your own food, just try to order what sounds good to you. "Please let me feel loved again" is better than "Bring him back to me." Other options include "Please show me how to heal my heart." "I wish to be free of this pain." "Please teach me to forgive." These are good, basic requests that will allow a master chef to serve you something that exceeds all expectations.

Requesting blessings is predicated on the assumption that great wisdom is already at work. This wisdom could be God, a deity, an angel, your own intelligence, or the quality of human goodness. It could also be something unnameable. It doesn't really matter what you call this wisdom. The only thing that seems required is not to quite understand what it is. I am a bit suspicious of anyone who claims to know with certainty just what this power is, where it lives, what it thinks, and the primary means of access to it. The moment I think that I understand the sacred oneness of existence, I've stepped outside of that oneness and therefore can't be trusted to explain it. So when you request blessings, no matter how certain you are of where and from whom they come, let there also be a little bit of not-knowing.

Dedicate the Merit

At the end of each practice session, you take the final and perhaps most important of the three steps that create sacred outlook and environment by dedicating the merit. In this strange, radical act, you give away whatever benefit you may have created for yourself when you made offerings and requested blessings. Period. I find this hard to do because I want to hang on to a tiny corner of goodness. I mean, for goodness' sake, why am I doing all of this if not to feel better?

I wish it worked that way—that you could go out and find something that would do you some good, bring it home, and then expect it to benefit you. That would be so simple. But when you go out and find something beneficial and then share it with everyone, this seems to magnify the benefit of everything. (Except perhaps the last cupcake.) So when you are finished with your spiritual practice, take a moment and reflect on whatever good may have been generated and offer it. If it helps, you can imagine all the countless beings in this world who are also suffering from a broken heart right now. Millions upon millions suffer just as you do, feeling the agony of acute loss. Ask in whatever way feels right to you that whatever you do to heal yourself be used to heal them as well. "I hope my spiritual practice can benefit others" is great, as is "I dedicate my practice for the benefit of others." Use words that feel natural and honest. Here is a traditional dedication of merit that is used in my Buddhist tradition:

> *By this merit may all attain omniscience.*
> *May it defeat the enemy, wrongdoing.*
> *From the stormy waves of birth, old age, sickness, and death*
> *May I free all beings.*
> *By the confidence of the golden sun of the great East,*
> *May the lotus garden of the Rigden's wisdom bloom.*
> *May the dark ignorance of sentient beings be dispelled.*
> *May all beings enjoy profound, brilliant glory.*

In between the first two steps (making an offering and requesting blessings) and the third (dedicating the merit) is the program itself where you are making friends with your broken heart and creating the space for it to heal. If you were to do the meditations and journaling exercises that comprise this program without these three steps, they would simply be psychological exercises—not without benefit, certainly. But you introduce a spiritual aspect and the possibility of connecting with great wisdom through these three very simple, very precious steps.

Beginning the Program

To prepare, create a place where you will make offerings. This will be your meditation spot, so there should also be room for a meditation cushion or a chair. A nice chair or cushion and small table are ideal, but you could also place a meditation cushion on the floor in front of a windowsill where the sun rises. Or you could dedicate a corner of your desk as the place of offering.

Gather some materials that signify offerings to you. Remember, what you are offering is symbolic of what is precious and ineffable, so choose things of beauty. They don't have to be expensive, but if you choose flowers, make sure they are fresh. If you choose a photograph of something or someone you love, put it in a nice frame. If you select scented candles, place them on a lovely dish or tray.

All you will need in addition to your meditation spot is a journal.

Choose a Friday date to start the program, or, if you don't work nine-to-five, during any seven-day period.

The Schedule

The first weekend, focus on making your life as quiet and simple as possible. You'll be spending as much time as possible by yourself with minimal interaction with others. So let family and friends know you'll be taking time for yourself. Cancel any social engagements. Make sure your kitchen is stocked so you won't have to think too much about food. Make a commitment to keep to a minimum all forms of entertainment: television, internet surfing, talking or texting with friends, reading fluff—as much as possible, don't engage in these things. If you're going to read, keep to subjects that relate to healing. The idea is to cut down on the amount of stimulus in your environment in order to allow your mind to quiet.

Friday Night
When you come home from work Friday night, set up your meditation area. Sometime in the evening, have a seat on your meditation chair or cushion with your journal for a brief journaling exercise. Settle down and take a moment just to sit there and appreciate wherever you are. What can you see, hear, smell? Noticing the space you're in is a simple way to come into the present moment.

Open your journal and finish these sentences:

Please help me to _____ so that I may _____.

Please guide me to _____ so that I may _____.

Please show me _____ so that I may _____.

Please teach me _____ so that I may _____.

Let these sentiments be your offering for tonight. Tear this page out of your journal, fold it up, and place it somewhere on your altar table.

Do Tranquility Meditation for ten minutes.

Dedicate the merit.

Saturday

Practice Tranquility Meditation in the morning for ten minutes. Get out your journal and write three longhand pages without censoring yourself. The pages don't have to make any sense. Just keep your hand moving across the page and, if the only thing you can think of to write is *Why am I doing this?* then write "Why am I doing this?" and fill up the pages. Let the words flow out onto the page. Then put them aside.

Sometime before lunch, pick up your journal again and settle yourself for a writing session that will last about an hour, or longer if you like. In this exercise you'll write the story of your relationship from a third-person perspective. Begin with this line: "They met like this." Then fill in how it happened. "They met like this: she was a bartender in a nightclub and he played guitar in the house band." Or "They met like this: she was in San Francisco for a business meeting with a new client who turned out to be the love of her life." Or "They met like this: they had known each other since high school but life circumstances had led them in different directions, until, one day, by coincidence, she ran into him at a party."

Continue from there. Write about how they felt about each other as they got to know each other. Did one of them develop romantic feelings first? Was one of them involved with someone else at the time? Was falling in love easy or fraught with difficulty? Did one develop romantic feelings before the other? How was this relationship different from her past relationships? How was it the same?

I know that "she" is you, but the point of this exercise is to step back from "her" and observe her behavior and emotions as the relationship developed. If you love to write, you can make this story superlong and detailed. If you do not like to write, just keep it simple. You can write the story in bullet points. If you feel like getting wildly creative, you can write the story in a dialogue or email exchange, a poem, or screenplay. Take it seriously, but have some fun with it.

When you think you've covered the early stages of the relationship—basically from the time you met or connected to the time you realized that you were in love—put the exercise aside for now. We'll be picking it up again later.

Now write on a corner of a piece of paper or Post-it note one to three things that you feel grateful to your ex for, things that arose during the early stages of the relationship. You could list things such as "I'm grateful to you for making me feel desirable" or "Thank you for that time I was stuck at the airport with a flight delay and you drove out just to keep me company" or "You were the first person ever to appreciate my sense of humor—thank you." When you've made your list, fold up the piece of paper and place it on your altar.

Close this writing session with ten minutes of meditation.

Have lunch.

Spend the rest of the afternoon reading, resting, doing little things around the house. Keep it very, very simple. Don't call friends. Don't go online. Keep your mental energy to yourself. This may feel uncomfortable at first, but you will adjust. If you cry a bunch, it's okay. If you don't, it's also okay.

Before dinner, do another ten-minute Tranquility session and spend the evening however you like. Again, keep it simple. Watch a movie that makes you laugh, but don't channel surf or text message your friends or go out clubbing. Keep your mind quiet and to yourself. Remember, the point of this weekend is to pacify turmoil and the simpler and quieter, the better.

Before going to sleep, return to your cushion for a few more minutes and dedicate the merit of your day. Using whatever words feel right to you, rouse a sense of the work you did, of all the effort you put in or were unable to put in on this day. Offer the fruit of your practice for the benefit of all beings, that everyone currently suffering the pain of a broken heart will be liberated, uplifted, and held in the cradle of loving-kindness.

As you drift off to sleep, reflect on your day, on all the feelings, words, insights, and frustrations you encountered. Allow a simple prayer to develop and offer this prayer to the loving spirits of the night. Ask them to guide you toward healing as you sleep. Sweet dreams.

Sunday

This second full day of inward focus and simplicity will proceed much as Saturday did. You'll continue practicing meditation, journaling, and writing out the story of your relationship. But on this evening we'll add a traditional Loving-Kindness Meditation practice.

Practice Tranquility Meditation in the morning for ten minutes. Get out your journal and write three longhand pages without censoring yourself.

Sometime before lunch, pick up your journal for the second part of your writing exercise. Move your characters forward into the middle segment of their relationship. You can begin with these sentences: "And so they settled into their relationship. They spent their time together doing things like _____. As they got to know each other, they came to see each other's good and bad qualities. What he loved about her was _____. What she loved about him was _____. On the other hand, what he didn't like about her was _____. What she didn't like about him was _____." And go from there. Describe several memorably wonderful times and several memorably not-so-wonderful times. If you fought, write about a particular fight. Describe the moments of particularly deep connection. Remember, it's your story; you're just writing it from a third party's point of view.

When you think you've covered the middle stages of the relationship, put the exercise aside for now. You should have covered the period between recognizing that you were in a relationship and the time things began to fall apart. Write about the relationship up to but not including this point. I know that it may be difficult to pinpoint this moment, so make your best effort. One or two incidents may stand out in your mind that you now know to be the beginning of the end, whether or not you knew it at the time.

Tear off another corner of a piece of paper or grab a Post-it note to close this writing exercise by writing one to three things that you feel grateful to your ex for, things that arose during the middle stages of the relationship. You could list things like "You taught me how to fight fair," or "When I lost my job, you were such a great friend," or "I know you made your best effort to be honest with me." When you've made your list, fold up the piece of paper and place it on your altar with the previous list. Meditate for ten minutes and then have lunch.

Spend the rest of the afternoon reading, resting, doing little things around the house.

Before dinner, do another ten-minute Tranquility session and spend the evening however you like. Remember: keep it simple.

Before going to sleep, return to your cushion and practice Loving-Kindness Meditation. Please refer to chapter 30 for specific instructions. As you begin the practice, check in with the qualities of your broken heart—how does it feel right now to have a broken heart? Let those feelings flood your heart. As you move through the phases of this practice—offering loving-kindness to a friend, a stranger, and an enemy—try to remain connected to this sense of brokenness and deep wish to love and be loved. When it's time to offer loving-kindness for all beings, offer it for all who struggle with heartbreak of any kind, whether it is related to romance or not. Finish by dedicating the merit of your day.

As you drift off to sleep, once again reflect on your day, on all the feelings, words, insights, and frustrations you encountered.

Allow a simple prayer to develop and offer this prayer to the loving spirits of the night. Ask them to guide you toward healing as you sleep.

Monday

If you are returning to your regular work life on Monday morning, set your alarm a bit earlier to give yourself time to practice Tranquility Meditation for ten minutes and write three longhand pages of free writing before heading out the door. These two activities should take about forty minutes.

During this entire week, try to keep your schedule as simple as possible. I know you can't avoid email, errands, and other responsibilities. That's okay. You can still get the full benefit of this program—just try not to take on any additional professional, scholastic, or social engagements during this time. Try to get home as quickly as you can after work so you can continue to work closely with your heart.

When you get home after the day is done, practice Tranquility for ten minutes. Then pick up your journal and finish your story. Write about the final third of your relationship. Begin with this prompt: "She knew the relationship had hit a rough patch when . . ." and then write about the first time she had an inkling that this wasn't going to work out. Describe some uncomfortable moments, big fights, or memorable emotional disconnects. Describe the breakup and end by completing this sentence: "When she realized it was over, she knew what she would miss about him, and what she would not" and describe those things. I know this may be painful. (Or not—there's no right way to feel.)

When you're finished with the story, once again, I'm going to ask you to write out one to three things that you are grateful, yes, grateful to him for that happened during this period. You could be grateful that he told the truth. You could be grateful that he showed his true colors. You could be grateful to him for having once loved you. You could be grateful that you no longer have to deal with one or two of the things that bugged you about him. Don't be snide, but be honest. So on a third scrap of paper or Post-it, write them down and place it on your altar with the other two slips of paper. Leave them there until the program ends. Finish the day with ten minutes of Tranquility and then dedicate the merit.

Tuesday–Thursday

Each of these days will follow the same schedule: ten minutes of Tranquility in the morning (or more if you like), followed by three pages of free writing. When you come home in the evening, do another ten-minute Tranquility session followed by Loving-Kindness practice. If you'd like, you could also contemplate and journal about one or all of these topics in the evenings:

- Going forward, how can I develop the ability to notice my habitual emotional reactions without necessarily *acting* on them? What helps me to tread the ground of powerful feelings without being overwhelmed by them or running away from them?
- How can I stop seeing others as devices for good or ill in my personal dramas? How can I learn to focus more on giving love than getting it?
- How can I come to terms with the idea that, somehow, all relationships end? What would help me to take a chance on love again, knowing there are no guarantees?
- If or when I enter into a new relationship, how could I bring the understanding I've gained from having a broken heart into it in a way that would make me a more loving person?

Close your day with ten minutes of Tranquility, dedicate the merit, and have a good night's sleep.

Friday

This final day of the program begins, once again, with ten minutes of Tranquility and three pages of free writing. When you return home in the evening, make sure, as much as possible, that you won't be disturbed. Sit in front of your shrine. Practice Tranquility for a few minutes, followed by Loving-Kindness. For this final session of Loving-Kindness, place your ex in each role during the practice—offer him loving-kindness as a loved one, as a stranger, and as an enemy. There are things you love or loved about him; bring those into your practice when you send loving-kindness to your "loved one." There are ways he is completely unknown to you, now and even when you were together. Picture him as a stranger to you during the "neutral person" part of the practice. And when it comes to the enemy portion, focus on the him who may have hurt or angered you. Finish by offering loving-kindness to all beings.

Sit for a few moments in silence, resting your mind on your breathing. Then gather the little pieces of paper with your words of gratitude. Using a fireproof bowl that is large enough to hold one scrap at a time without catching your house on fire, put the first list you made in there and burn it. Then the second list, and finally the third one. As these papers burn, acknowledge that, no matter what happens in the future, right now, this relationship is over. And you are a stronger, more beautiful person for having welcomed it into your life, experienced it, and watched it dissolve.

To close, let it all go, all of it. Practice Tranquility for ten minutes in a state of openness and freedom.

Now revisit the questions you answered at the very beginning of this book. Have your answers changed? What do these changes mean to you? How would you describe the journey you've been on? I've added a few additional questions at the end.

1. My breakup occurred _____ days/months/ years ago and since that time, my primary emotions have been _____, _____, and _____.

2. The last time I felt feelings such as these was when _____. What I notice when I compare these two experiences is _____. (If you've never experienced heartbreak before, leave blank.)

3. The thing that has been the most difficult for me since this relationship ended is _____.

4. When I think about our breakup, the thought or thoughts that plague(s) me over and over is/are _____ _____.

5. I feel the pain of this loss most acutely when I _____ _____.

6. What I miss most about our relationship is _____ _____.

7. What I don't miss about our relationship is _____ _____.

8. The thing I regret most is _____.

9. The unforeseen benefit of this breakup is _____ _____.

10. If I could take him back right now, I would/would not and here's why: _____.

11. What I have discovered about myself is _____ _____.

12. What I have discovered about my friends is _____ _____.

13. The most important thing I have to say about love is _____.

14. If I could tell everyone in the world who has a broken heart one thing, it would be _____.

15. The most important thing I need to tell myself right now is _____.

Dedicate the merit. Congratulations. You are now a spiritual warrior.

After the Program

The best way to stabilize and deepen the impact of the program is to continue your meditation practice. If you can also continue the three pages of longhand writing per day, the seeds of healing and insight that were planted during the program will continue to blossom. If you're not sure you want to make either of these practices a part of your daily life, try to continue doing one or both for at least a few days so the program ending won't feel too abrupt. Let it taper off gradually. But I strongly urge you to continue both of these wonderful practices at least until you feel you're out of the acute stage of heartache. I promise that you will be glad you did.

Afterword

In the beginning, I took the teacher as teacher,
In the middle, I took the scriptures as teacher,
In the end, I took my own mind as teacher.

—Dilgo Khyenste Rinpoche, *Journey to Enlightenment*

WHEN I FINALLY fell in love with the right person and got married, I was happy for a variety of reasons, including that I would never have to date again. I believed that the days of emotional roller-coaster rides were over. On one hand, the biggest hand, I was so relieved. But on the other, subtler hand, I guess I was a little worried. What would take the place of all that intensity that sometimes felt so awful—and sometimes felt so gooood? I mean, when a relationship is new, you stand together at the edge of heartbreak, not knowing where it's all going, unsure of whether or not you really fit together, feeling enraptured one moment and terrified the next. Although you feel like throwing up all the time, you also feel pretty alive. It's exhilarating and also completely nerve-racking. The possibility of imminent heartbreak really keeps you on your toes.

Well, I needn't have worried that my days of potential heartbreak were over. In many ways, marriage is the greatest heartbreak of all. There is no end to the uncertainty, cycles of difficulty followed by rapprochement, and discomfort of intimacy.

If heartbreak is a continual opening to deeper and deeper levels of love, if it means unsheathing your heart and opening the gates wide so that your heart is available to everyone, then marriage itself is the ideal crucible because rather than lessening emotional vulnerability, it is one continuous heartbreak. Hey, this is good news! It's weird news, but it's good, nonetheless.

The more deeply you love, the more closely you feel the possibility of loss. It's really true that loving something or someone dearly is the most vulnerable position you can ever find yourself in. On one hand, you are filled with indescribable joy and gratitude for such incredible good fortune. On the other hand, you could lose it. This is totally true. And P.S., you will, whether by falling out of love, finding a new love, or, of course, by death. When I think of how much I love my sweet husband, almost simultaneously arises the thought that one of us will die first and someday we will have to bear taking leave of each other. Honestly, I think this is why relationships are so difficult, not because someone isn't ambitious enough or is a slob or demands too much or whatever. These things are minuscule compared to acknowledging that what you have so painstakingly searched for will eventually disappear; no matter how carefully and beautifully you build your castle together, one day it will simply wash out to sea. This is how it is.

It's so very, very hard to bear this but it must be understood in order for love to blossom fully. I mean, there are two choices here: acknowledge the impermanence of who and what you love so you can accurately appreciate and value the profound and precious gift you have received . . . or try as hard as you can never to think about such a thing (or imagine that if it ever does happen, it will be so far into the future that maybe you won't even like each other anymore) and, as a couple, go into emotional lockdown, refusing to acknowledge love's path, and thereby fail to value it altogether—which eventually will result in its demise. It's as simple as this: if you try to hold on to it in a static form (and who doesn't want to freeze the perfect moment?), you kill it. It's so unfunnily ironic that when you find love, you also find the sorrow of impermanence.

Committing to marriage is therefore committing to a life of sadness and faith, inseparable from each other. Sadness, because, duh, it's just sad that you're both going to die. And faith, because without knowing how or why you have to do this, you must do it. You must honor love wherever or however it appears and give yourself to it wholeheartedly. Why? I do not know. This is the faith part.

Sometimes when we're falling asleep, Duncan and I lie on our sides and look at each other. I touch his face or he touches mine. I don't know what he's thinking, but I'm thinking something like, *I love this person. I love him, I just do, even almost ten years later. I don't even know why anymore, particularly. He is indescribably precious to me and all the loving things and all the icky things that happen between us just seem to deepen our relationship because there is some kind of love-glue holding us together and I don't even know what it's made of or how we got so lucky. So. Lucky.* But when I try to hold on to this moment of love, it is gone before I can capture it and I just have to watch it dissolve. It's very painful. There is nothing to hold on to. Somehow, this is the way love works.

But other times I just look at him and think, *Wow, he really needs a shave* or *Did he wear the same socks today that he wore yesterday?* You just never know.

Ironically, I think that often people get married because they want to put a stop to this process, to love itself. Enough already with the deepening and the tenderness and the vulnerability. Okay, okay, so it's a sign of spiritual awareness, but how much can one person take? I just want to find the right person, settle down, and take it easy. I'm willing to retire all that "excitement" and get real. Well, this actually never happens. Never, ever. Unless, and there's one big exception, you both agree to shut your hearts down. You implicitly or explicitly come to some agreement about how a wife or husband or partner should act and then stick with it by modulating your emotional life in service to this pattern, and not to love itself. Then, yes, your heart will not break. Because it will be dead and only what is living can be broken.

So, it's a spiritual path, whether you like it or not. (Sometimes I do; sometimes I don't.) All those hokey books and articles that say, "Oh, relationships are a spiritual path" (as if that's supposed to make things better) are true, I'm totally sad to say. A relationship *is* a path.

For me, in becoming a Buddhist, I learned just how true this was. The same pitfalls and joys that come from working with a spiritual teacher also occur in marriage. I can see the parallels in the way both relationships—with my husband and with my spiritual teacher—have developed. They're not that different. They are both profound teachers.

Relationships are lonely. My relationship with my husband is lonely. My relationship with my teacher is lonely. They're the same kind of lonely—I have no idea what either of them is really talking about. And these are the good relationships. I really love them both, but in both cases the relationship is planted somewhere just outside my capacity for understanding. The only thing I know is that I'm no longer in a relationship with a person (husband or teacher). I'm in a relationship with a relationship that doesn't really care what I have to say. It has its own life. So I just wait for it to tell me what to do.

The other day my husband and I had a fight. It was a bad one. Super bad. Bad like leaving-the-house-at-1:00-a.m.-to-go-sleep-on-the-couch-in-my-office bad. It's so clichéd to say that I can't even remember what it was about, but I sort of can't. Well, maybe I can, but just don't want to believe that something so unbelievably stupid (someone not telling someone else that she bought a new camera . . . I mean, it only cost two hundred dollars and I needed it for work) could cause two normally sane people to absolutely lose their minds and jump up and down yelling at each other about who is responsible with money and who is not.

I was so depressed by this argument, I could hardly sleep. I dragged myself home at 6:00 a.m., dreading seeing him, but also hoping I would so he could see that I was still ignoring him. As I let myself in and walked up the stairs to our bedroom, he was exiting the shower, towel around his waist. His hair was wet and smelled like drugstore pineapple. His bare chest looked kind of dewy and sweet, not at all like the chest of someone you'd hate. Although I was still angry, I could see that he no longer was. (When he blows up in anger, his emotions metabolize and become digestible—he feels better after a "good" fight. For me, a fight is like getting socked in the head, the kind of punch that at first you can't even feel how much it hurts and then throbs for days.)

He came toward me and held his palms up in an unreadable

gesture. My palms spontaneously rose to mirror his, whether to stop him from coming closer or to hold him to me, I also couldn't tell. Back off. Come here. It didn't matter which one I did, because in that moment I realized I was trapped. I couldn't push him away nor could I hold him close enough. I couldn't keep him at bay because our lives are no longer two separate but parallel tracks as they were when we began living together. No. We're living one life together. I don't know at what moment this happened, but something invisible pushed us into a single life. We must have held each other one too many times. Inhaled each other's breaths while falling asleep one too many times. Had the same fight, kissed the same kiss, exchanged the same glance, eaten off the same plate one too many damn times. Our bodies and hearts have reformed into cutouts that can hold only the other. From this realization and from the sight of his bare chest and the scent of his pineapple hair, I wanted to open to him, to hold him close just because for whatever mysterious reason, the mere sight of him touches me so much. Even when I don't really like him.

But no embrace will ever really satisfy. I could never hold him close enough for him to actually know me; he would never know what it felt like for me to do this, why I was doing it, or to recognize the sequence of thoughts and feelings that led to this opening. I saw the depth of our connection and the simultaneous inability to know each other. *He must feel the same exact way,* I thought as I pulled him close. Very lonely. And, I realized, the closer we got, the more shocking and painful it would be still to not really know each other.

In my spiritual practice as a Buddhist, I've been encouraged to open myself to spiritual wisdom, to the kind of knowing that goes beyond the conventional mind. I've made a commitment to this effort and have taken many vows, committed to demanding meditation practices, and even found a teacher, something I had always scoffed at as an excuse made by the lily-livered to forego adult responsibility. But when you find your teacher, it isn't all that different from finding your husband. On one hand, you are bowled over by the extraordinary fact of their very existence and how profoundly and unquestioningly you love them, but on the other hand, during the first-blush phase, you look at them and go, "That's it?"

Still, as both relationships progress, your beloved becomes both more familiar and more inscrutable as time goes on. You question the vows you made. Some days they seem outrageous, impossible (I said I'd always love *you*?), and on others their true meaning deepens beyond what you had originally imagined.

If the marriage vow is to love, the vow to the teacher is to open yourself to his instruction and influence. It's very scary. But here's the funny part. It's much more complicated than doing one hundred Hail Marys or one hundred thousand prostrations just because he told you to. At some point the teacher enters your mind. It's impossible to describe this. It begins with simply recalling his verbal instructions when you sit down to do your meditation practice ("Make awareness itself the object of your meditation"), then graduates to unbidden reminders as you go through the day (you're about to give the finger to the guy who just cut you off in traffic, but suddenly remember your teacher saying, "Regard all beings as your mother," which is a teacher's way of saying, "Please don't flip people off").

But at some point you stop hearing the teacher speak to you in his voice and you start hearing him speak in yours. What seems to happen is, because he is your teacher, you have somehow always known him. It's sort of like, as a grown-up still hearing your mother's voice when you're about to take the last piece of pie ("Haven't you already had two pieces?"), except he says things such as "Regard all dharmas as dreams" and "The mind is empty and luminous." The more you relax your mind and the more you practice, the more kinds of wisdom energies begin to manifest themselves in your existence. These energies are variously described as self-existing wisdom, Buddhas of wisdom, bodhisattvas of compassion, and, of course, as Susan Piver, if you happen to be Susan Piver.

But are the Buddhas and bodhisattvas really there? Do they know me? How will I ever know them? Am I inviting them or rejecting them? I have no idea. Sometimes I think I'm in a relationship with them; sometimes I don't. I can feel that the longer I practice, the more something happens, but I'm not really sure what that something is. I used to simply go to dharma talks and then try to practice what I'd been taught. I still try to do this. But just as often, these days I get my practice instructions from Aerosmith songs or an overheard conversation on the train. There's nothing mysterious about it—I'm just listening to my iTunes or going to work and suddenly something clicks, like, "It's really true—I don't exist." I don't know where it comes from. Everything starts to sound like the teacher's voice, and all I know is that my efforts to connect more deeply with him have become much more dream-like and difficult to differentiate from my own mind. It's very personal. Intimate. Lonely. Just like my husband stepping out of the shower with pineapple dewdrops in his hair, my teacher steps out of my own mind stream, palms held up in an equally in-scrutable gesture. Communications are taking place in a way I no longer understand. These two individuals have taken root within my mind and speak to me in their own curious language, using my mind as their voice. Some days I can make out what they're saying, and on others it sounds like complete gibberish. The last thing I can share with either of them is what it's like to be with them. It's just too intimate to describe. Both relationships are teaching me something, but I can no longer understand the instructions. Still, learning occurs.

Recently I was talking to friend of mine, also a practitioner, but from a different lineage. He was telling me that, nowadays, his meditation practice consists of getting up in the morning, going to his cushion, and just sitting there. He basically tries not to do any-thing at all. To deepen his understanding of the teachings, there are no longer any rules to follow, such as "Place attention on the breath" or "Visualize an open sky." Just like me, he doesn't really know what to do anymore. He can't go back to following a set of practice instructions, nor is there a new set to jump forward into. There is only space and the feeling of groundlessness. In his tradi-tion, he says, this stage of spiritual development is called "stupefac-tion." This is where no one can tell you what to do anymore, no one but your teacher, who somehow can never be found, yet is every-where.

All I can do is listen, without knowing what listening looks like. Some kind of dialogue is taking place beyond my radar. No one will ever know what this is like for me. Not even me. All I can do is allow both of them to break my heart, over and over again. And see what happens next.

Appendix A

The "I'm About to Totally Freak Out"
Checklist of Alternatives

Here is a list of things you could do when you think you're about to lose it. It's meant for those superacute moments when you basically can't even remember your own name and you just need someone to give you a task. It is a semiserious list divided into three categories (distract, indulge, fight) of things you could do instead of drunk dialing, head shaving, burning things down, or devouring many cakes at one sitting. I can personally attest to the viability of these items to take my mind off what ails me, even if it's only for a few minutes. Refer to this list when you are desperate for something, anything to do to distract, indulge, or fight against your sorrow.

Distract It

- Dump every single item of clothing you own on the floor and divide into two piles: things that make you feel attractive and things that don't. Take the latter pile to Goodwill.
- Organize your Netflix queue.
- Go to Amazon.com, Goodreads.com, or Shelfari.com and review all the relationship books you've ever read; begin dialogue with like-minded readers. Make your suggested reading list for others who are going through heartbreak.

- Organize your iPod playlists.
- Identify five to seven DVDs that do not make you cry. These could be funny movies or just absorbing ones. Keep this stack handy, and when you feel yourself start to hyperventilate, pop one in the player.

My List:
The 40 Year Old Virgin
Anchorman: The Legend of Ron Burgundy
All About Eve
The Flight of the Conchords (Okay, this series is the funniest thing I have EVER seen.)
His Girl Friday
Intolerable Cruelty
Out of the Past
The Lady Eve
The Wire (any season)
The Women (original version)
Any movie with a fashion show or makeover

I queried friends and these were on their lists:
Battlestar Galactica
The Big Lebowski
Bowfinger
Coming to America
Dodgeball
Love Actually
Mulan
Office Space
The Princess Bride
Raising Arizona

- Popular lore (now debunked) has it that Eskimos have countless names for snow, perhaps because snow is what they live in. Heartbroken folks live in a world of tears. Make up names for different kinds of crying. To get you started, here are a few kinds of crying that should have their own names:

Sobbing without tears
When you feel like crying, but you can't—no tears come out
Crying that overtakes you out of the blue
Crying in your sleep
You don't even know you're crying
Talking and crying at the same time
You're so sad that the person you're talking to starts crying,
      even though you aren't

- If you haven't already, start following people on Twitter.com. I love Twitter, which is a social networking site that enables you to instant message with people all over the world. (Follow me! twitter.com/spiver.) Someone coined the phrase "ambient intimacy" to describe Twitter and that is just right. To experience it, log on to the site, create a user identity, find people, and start "following" them. Right now, millions of people are chatting with each other 24/7—but only in 140-character increments, which is what Twitter limits you to, so no one can get overly verbose. It's like a cocktail party that's always going on, and it enables you to get and give some human contact whenever you want. And disappear when you want. Any time of the day or night you can find someone to talk to.

Indulge It

- Identify five to seven DVDs that do make you cry. I'm not talking about those dark, gloomy movies that just make you depressed—I'm talking about the ones that make you bawl like a baby. Sometimes it's a comedy and sometimes it's *Bambi* or a reality TV show. For example, the television show *What Not to Wear* always makes me cry even though it's just a fashion show that shows women how to dress to suit their size, shape, age, etc. (Sometimes about how they always see themselves as beautiful in the end . . .) Keep this stack handy, and when you just need to let it all out, pop one in and sob with dignity.

My List:
A Beautiful Mind
Dark Victory
Field of Dreams
Gladiator
The Last Samurai
Stranger Than Fiction (when Will Ferrell sings "Whole Wide
   World")
Anything where a dog dies

I queried friends (on Twitter, actually!) and these were on
their lists:
Bambi
Big Fish
Dead Poets Society
E.T.: The Extraterrestrial
Fiddler on the Roof
Grave of the Fireflies (Hotaru no haka)
The Green Mile
Hotel Rwanda
I Am Sam
Life Is Beautiful
The Lion King
The Little Mermaid
Million Dollar Baby
The Notebook
Philadelphia
The Sisterhood of the Traveling Pants
Steel Magnolias
Sweet November
Titanic
Whale Rider

• Make a sob-sister playlist and listen to it. Here are my top ten
songs for when I want to get all worked up. (You can go to my website to hear them, susanpiver.com/WOBH_songs.)

"A Change Is Gonna Come" (Sam Cooke)
"The Dark End of the Street" (James Carr)
"I Can't Stand the Rain" (Ann Peebles)
"I Can't Stop Loving You" (Freddy Fender)
"I've Been Loving You Too Long" (Otis Redding)
"There Is an End" (The Greenhornes, with Holly Golightly)
"What Becomes of the Brokenhearted" (Jimmy Ruffin)
"When I Get Like This" (The Five Royales)
"Whole Wide World" (Wreckless Eric)
"For Your Precious Love" (Jerry Butler)

Fight It

- For god's sake, go to the gym.
- Take on an exercise regimen you think you can't do: If you're a yogini, try a forty-five-minute walk/run instead. If you're a runner, go to a yoga class. If you always take spinning, try strength training. If you don't do anything, do something.
- Walk. Walk. Walk. Drop everything and take a walk when you feel yourself about to collapse. You can walk in the morning or you can walk at night (if you don't live in a scary neighborhood). You can take a break from your desk and walk around the block. You can walk in the summer and you can walk in the winter. There's something incredibly cozy and fun about piling on coats, scarves, and hats and taking yourself for a walk when normal people would stay inside (when it's raining or snowing, for example). You are not a normal person right now. Go with it.
- Help a stranger. This may be the most time-worn suggestion of all time, but it works. The very second you help someone in need, something completely magical happens. All the energy that you had been devoting to propping yourself up turns from half-assed to raging, a force to be reckoned with—when it's aimed at someone else. Self-hatred, depression, and insecurity disappear when you put yourself in the service of another. Everything you wish you could do for yourself—take your mind off it, recover your dignity, feel good about yourself, become energized—just happens. You can help someone by:

Giving him or her money: do some research and donate to a charity. Go a little out of your comfort zone. If you could afford $10, give $15. If you could afford $500, give $750. And so on.

Volunteering: to read to people in the hospital, help out at an animal shelter, for a politician you admire, or at your church. One of the best tools I ever found for working with my depression was to volunteer at a crisis center. Talking to others in crisis balanced me out, for some reason. The best kind is when you get right up in there with people (or animals) who are in actual pain, whether physical or emotional. Let their difficulty into your heart. You'll know what to do next. And the volunteer agency will train you, too.

Calling them: you can also help people you already know. Call a friend or family member who is going through some difficulty. Don't talk about yourself. Keep the focus of the conversation on him or her.

When you turn the attention away from your suffering and instead try to help others with their own, far from being a sacrifice, it becomes as healing (or more) for you than it is for them.

Appendix B

Instructions for Creating a
Daily Meditation Practice

If you want to begin a regular meditation practice, I commend you wholeheartedly. For me (and for millions of people over the past several thousand years), a regular meditation practice creates the foundation for other things in my life to work properly. Even though it seems impossible for you to add one more "to-do" to what is a list already careening out of control, this to-do makes all the others doable. Here are some suggestions for making meditation a part of your everyday life, as best you can.

The most important thing to consider first is finding a credentialed, experienced meditation instructor to help guide your practice. All that this means is someone who has practiced longer than you and who is affiliated with a genuine, time-tested, bona fide spiritual lineage. Basically, anything over 2,500 years old will do. The Shambhala Buddhist lineage provides meditation instructors for free, and we are trained quite rigorously. Call your local center and request one and they will match you up with someone. You could meet with this person every month or so, just to review how your practice is going. When you assign yourself the task of watching your own mind, it can get a little claustrophobic or confusing and it's helpful to have someone to consult with.

In addition to the Shambhala lineage, you could try to find a

Zen center or an Insight Meditation (or Vipassana) group in your town. These are completely wonderful traditions—I don't want you to think I'm shilling on behalf of my own lineage alone. See the resources at the back of this book for help in locating a meditation instructor in these lineages.

The next most important thing to note is that consistency is more important than duration when it comes to your meditation practice. In other words, ten minutes once a day is preferable to sixty minutes once a week. That said, the more the better, but most important is to establish routine at the outset, one that is doable for you. Try to meditate at the same time every day. This helps create a new habit.

I suggest *not* saying to yourself anything like "From this day forth I will meditate every single day of my life, period." This is like punching a one-way ticket to Palookaville and you want to avoid this. I'm a big fan of taking only one manageable step at a time. Instead of making a lifelong commitment to something you have not done before, try making a one-month commitment and see how that goes. "I will meditate every day for one month" is something you can do—or one week, one year, and so on. Aim for a time frame that is about 25 percent beyond your comfort zone— not 250 percent or –25 percent. It should be for a period that, when you complete it, you feel a real sense of accomplishment. Ten minutes per day for one month is usually good. If you feel tempted to meditate for fifteen or twenty minutes, don't. If you feel tempted to meditate less, try to avoid this, too. The idea is to connect with a groove and be precise about it.

Once you've decided on a time frame, choose a good meditation spot. I have a little shrine and sitting area in my office at home. I know people who have set aside an entire room just for meditation, and I also know those who sit up in bed and, bingo, they're in their meditation room. One kind of person does not have a better practice than the other—what counts more than anything is discipline and devotion to the technique.

Create a quiet, relaxed spot to meditate. Find something to sit on that suits you, which could be a chair or meditation cushion. If space is at a premium, you could simply designate a particular chair as your meditation spot. To prepare the space for meditation, make sure it's clean and neat. Find a timer of some sort. You could use an alarm clock or a stick of incense. (If you like incense, burn a stick and time how long it takes to finish. If it takes twenty minutes to burn completely and you've decided to practice for twenty minutes, you're in great shape. If ten, stop practicing when it's halfway burned.) See Resources (appendix C) "Meditation Supplies" for where to acquire such things. If you'd like, you can light a candle or place a photo of something or someone inspiring nearby, but these things are not necessary. Keep it simple.

As mentioned, try to practice at the same time each day. Most people find it simplest to meditate in the mornings, but some prefer evenings. Don't beat yourself up if you miss a day. The only thing worse than not doing what you know you should is making yourself feel terrible about not doing what you know you should.

What would you guess are the biggest impediments to meditation practice? I assumed they were not having enough time or being unable to relax. According to meditation experts, there are three classic obstacles to a meditation practice. The first one is called "forgetting the instructions." We don't forget because we're dumb, we just forget because we haven't ingrained the moves yet. It's like learning to play a piece of music. Learning it once doesn't guarantee that the next time you sit down to play, you'll remember all the details. It's the same with meditation. So it's really helpful to prepare by reviewing the instructions, either by running down them in your mind or rereading them in this or another book. In addition to refreshing your memory, before you practice take a moment and say to yourself, *Now I'm going to practice meditation. During this time, everything can wait.* Tell yourself this a few times before beginning your practice, or until you basically feel that it's true.

The technical term for obstacle number two is laziness. There are three kinds of laziness. The first is the regular kind, which I don't even have to explain, but it involves such things as watching TV instead of meditating. The second kind is called "becoming disheartened," considered a form of laziness because you have ceased to value your own agenda. Stop that! The final kind of laziness is actually being too busy. If you think about it, a schedule that is too full to allow for peace, quiet, and self-care is a sign that someone's dropped the ball. So when you sense any of these qualities afoot, snoozing, losing heart, and speediness, raise the red flag and try to get back to your meditation cushion.

The third obstacle is just as interesting as the first two. It's called "Laxity/Elation." Laxity is when you're too mentally dull to meditate with precision and you fall asleep on the cushion a lot. Elation is getting carried away by interesting experiences that may arise during meditation practice. Insights and positive emotional shifts are fabulous, not to be discounted—however, while on your meditation cushion you aim to let go of both laxity and elation in order to come back to the rise and fall of breath. So don't get carried away by either and think, *I'll never be able to do this,* or *I must now be a world-class meditator.* Both are distractions that should be labeled "thinking" just before you return your attention to your breath.

Most important of all is to be kind to yourself. So when you make time to sit, relax, and when you fail to make time, relax about that, too. Just try again the next day.

When you are done practicing for the day, take a moment before rising to wish that all beings everywhere could somehow also benefit from your practice session.

So, to recap, the instructions for creating a daily meditation practice are:

1. Find a meditation instructor to share your experiences with.
2. Make a time commitment that is doable and be consistent about it.
3. Create a good environment for your practice.
4. Put aside everything but your practice for the time you are on the cushion.
5. Review the instructions before sitting.
6. Avoid the three forms of laziness: regular, becoming disheartened, being too busy.
7. Try not to let either laxity or elation carry you away.

8. Be kind to yourself.
9. Close your practice by dedicating the merit.

I truly wish you all the benefits of a regular meditation practice, which are numerous and profound. Most of all, I hope that this practice will enable you to recognize the extraordinary heart-opening that also occurs when the heart is broken, and, rather than finding a way to close it again, to stabilize your heart in this state of openness.

A p p e n d i x   C

Resources

BOOKS

On Meditation
John Daido Loori
Finding the Still Point: A Beginner's Guide to Zen Meditation
Shambhala Publications

Sakyong Mipham
Turning the Mind into an Ally
Riverhead Books

Larry Rosenberg
Breath by Breath: The Liberating Practice of Insight Meditation
Shambhala Publications

Shunryu Suzuki
Zen Mind, Beginner's Mind
Shambhala Publications

Tulku Thondup
The Healing Power of Mind
Shambhala Publications

Chögyam Trungpa
Cutting Through Spiritual Materialism
Shambhala Publications

Applied Meditation: Mindfulness in Everyday Life
Tsultrim Allione
Feeding Your Demons: Ancient Wisdom for Resolving Inner Conflict
Harper San Francisco

Pema Chödrön
The Places that Scare You
When Things Fall Apart
Shambhala Publications

Thich Nhat Hanh
Peace Is Every Step: The Path of Mindfulness in Everyday Life
Bantam Books

Byron Katie
Loving What Is: Four Questions That Can Change Your Life
Harmony Books

Dalai Lama
The Art of Happiness: A Handbook for Living
Riverhead Books

Sakyong Mipham
Ruling Your World: Ancient Strategies for Modern Life
Morgan Road Books

Shunryu Suzuki (author), Edward Espe Brown (editor)
Not Always So: Practicing the True Spirit of Zen
HarperCollins

Chögyam Trungpa
Shambhala: The Sacred Path of the Warrior
Shambhala Publications

Jon Kabat-Zinn
*Wherever You Go, There You Are: Mindfulness Meditation in
    Everyday Life*
Hyperion

On Meditation and the Brain
Richard J. Davidson (editor), Anne Harrington (editor)
*Visions of Compassion: Western Scientists and Tibetan Buddhists
    Examine Human Nature*
Oxford University Press

Daniel Goleman
Destructive Emotions: A Scientific Dialogue with the Dalai Lama
Bantam Books

Rinpoche Yongey Mingyur
The Joy of Living: Unlocking the Secret and Science of Happiness
Harmony Books

On Loving Kindness Meditation
Pema Chödrön
No Time to Lose: A Timely Guide to the Way of the Bodhisattva
Shambhala Publications

Sharon Salzberg
*A Heart As Wide as the World: Stories on the Path of Loving-
    kindness*
Lovingkindness: The Revolutionary Art of Happiness
Shambhala Publications

Santideva
The Way of the Bodhisattva
Shambhala Publications

Chögyam Trungpa
Training the Mind and Cultivating Loving-Kindness
Shambhala Publications

MEDITATION TEACHERS

To find a Shambhala center and meditation instructor near you:
shambhala.org

Other recommended meditation schools:
Vipassana: Insight Meditation Society
dharma.org/ims/

Zen: San Francisco Zen Center (affiliated groups)
sfzc.org/zc/maps.asp?catid=1,11

MEDITATION RETREAT CENTERS

Shambhala Mountain Center
Red Feather Lakes, Colo.
shambhalamountain.org

Kármê Chöling Shambhala Meditation Center
Barnet, Vt.
karmecholing.org

Dechen Choling
Limoges, France
dechencholing.org

MEDITATION SUPPLIES

Free meditation timer download:
http://wcrawford.org/2006/11/09/meditation-timer-12/

For meditation cushions, shrine tables, and other supplies:
DharmaCrafts
dharmacrafts.com

Samadhi Cushions
samadhicushions.com

Ziji
ziji.com

BLOGROLL

Integral Options Café
integral-options.blogspot.com

Jonathan Foust: Serving Humanity Since 1956
jonathanfoust.com

Monkey Mind
monkeymindonline.blogspot.com

Numinous Nonsense
vincenthorn.com

Sarahcentric
Sarahcentric.com

Shambhala Sun Magazine
shambhalasun.com

Reverend Danny Fisher
chaplaindanny.blogspot.com/

The Interdependence Project
theidproject.com

The Worst Horse
theworsthorse.com/

Tricycle: The Buddhist Review
tricycle.com

Welcome to the Mingdom
shambloga.blogspot.com

ONLINE MEDITATION INSTRUCTION

Sakyong Mipham
Learning to Meditate
mipham.com/videos.php?id=3

PODCASTS

Buddhist Geeks
personallifemedia.com/podcasts/236-buddhist-geeks

The Interdependence Project Podcast
theidproject.com/podcast.htm

ZenCast
amberstar.libsyn.com/

Acknowledgments

At some point during the writing of this book, I had meaningful conversation about its content with, and/or felt the kind support of, the following lovely people. Whether intending to or not, a piece of each one's heart found its way onto these pages. I thank them for their insight and friendship.

Dominick Anfuso
Josh Baran
Sari Boren
Maya Breuer
Edward Espe Brown
Michael Carroll
Richard Faulds
Crystal Gandrud
Carolyn Gimian
Beth Grossman
Alexander 't Hart
Joel Heller
Daniel Hessey
Sarah Jackson
Leonard Jacobs

Christopher Kilmer
Adam Lobel
Frank Linn
Ming-Lien Linsley
Melanie Lowe
Catherine MacCoun
Cindy Matchett
Larry Mermelstein
Patricia Reinstein
Eden Steinberg
Dana Strong
Jim and Kathy Tolstrup
Lila Kate Wheeler

While writing this book, I read works by the following and took much inspiration from them:

Karen Armstrong
Pema Chödrön
Dzongsar Jamyang Khyentse
Sakyong Mipham Rinpoche
Longchen Rabjam
Tulku Thondup
Chögyam Trunpga

I thank my meditation students, who demonstrate again and again the truth of the dharma through their practice. I also thank those who have attended my writers' retreats, for being a source of inspiration and joy.

Thank you to Cassell and Karl Gross (and Bussi) for the chance to work out of their spectacular home in the Rocky Mountains, where this book really took shape.

My agent, Stephanie Tade, shepherded this book with such sensitivity and encouraged me in just the right ways. In fact, the book was her idea. I was thinking of writing an article called "The Wisdom of a Broken Heart," and she said, "Hey, that would make a great book!" And here we are. I am grateful to her for her kindness, clarity, and courage, and for being my dharma sister.

Thank you to my wonderful editor at Free Press, Leslie Meredith. She loved this book idea from the start, which gave me tremendous confidence. She is as kind as she is clear and did a fantastic job of honoring my voice while always keeping the focus on the needs of the reader—making this book more helpful to actual humans who are suffering, which was basically the entire point to begin with.

Enduring gratitude to Derek O'Brien for breaking and healing my heart in untold ways. May we be intertwined for many lifetimes. To quote the great Otis Rush, my love will never die.

Much gratitude to soul sister number one, Emily Bower, for her continuing encouragement, wisdom, and love. She has the magic ability to pick me up when I'm down and help me see the world with fresh eyes.

Special thanks to Emily Sell for our conversations in her room at Shambhala Mountain Center and beyond about structure, voice, and view, which were like shining a light in darkness. When I saw the book through her eyes, I saw it clearly. She offered excellent editorial and sangha-sisterly insight (and chocolate) at precisely the right moments.

I am extremely grateful to Tulku Thondup for helping me enter more deeply into my spiritual path, and for his teachings on Medicine Buddha practice, which were indispensable.

To my deeply esteemed *kalyanamitra,* I offer gratitude beyond measure for your impeccable outer, inner, and secret guidance. And love. You know who you are.

Although we never met in this lifetime, I meet the Druk Sakyong, Chögyam Trungpa Rinpoche, at every turn. His writings make my life make sense, and infuse my practice and study with ordinary magic. This book is my attempt to meet his mind.

Only by attaining absolute enlightenment could I express sufficient gratitude for the love and generosity of my root teacher, the Sakyong Mipham, Jampal Trinley Dradul Rinpoche. May your lotus feet remain planted for an ocean of kalpas.

And to my beloved husband, Duncan, I owe inexpressible gratitude for supporting me with his whole heart. I am so thankful for the grace with which he accepted my lengthy physical and emotional absences while writing this book and still managed the strength and certainty to carry me over hurdles I certainly would not have cleared on my own.

About the Author

Susan Piver is a writer, teacher, and speaker on topics such as love, creativity, and spirituality. She is the *New York Times* bestselling author of *The Hard Questions: 100 Essential Questions to Ask Before You Say "I Do"* and the award-winning *How Not to Be Afraid of Your Own Life*, chosen as best spiritual book of 2007 by Books for a Better Life. Susan leads Authentic Inspiration: A Retreat for Writers, a workshop specifically designed for creative flow, and The Wisdom of a Broken Heart, a weekend workshop exploring the ideas in this book. She has written for *Body & Soul, SELF, O: The Oprah Magazine,* and the *Shambhala Sun* and is regularly featured in the media, including multiple appearances on *Oprah*, the *Today* show, CNN, and in *USA Today, The Wall Street Journal, Time, Money*, and others. Susan has been a student of Buddhism since 1995 and graduated from a Buddhist seminary in 2004. She is an authorized meditation instructor in the Shambhala Buddhist lineage.

For more information on her books, workshops, newsletters, and online courses, please visit susanpiver.com.

susan@susanpiver.com
twitter.com/spiver
facebook.com/susan.piver

By the confidence of the golden sun of the great East,
May the lotus garden of the Rigden's wisdom bloom.
May the dark ignorance of sentient beings be dispelled.
May all beings enjoy profound, brilliant glory.

Ki Ki So So Ashe Lha Gyal Lo
Tak Seng Kyung Druk Di Yar Kye!

CPSIA information can be obtained
at www.ICGtesting.com
Printed in the USA
BVHW031120040623
665288BV00001BA/1